GRACE, LOVE, AND

SOME FOOTBALL

Zach Mitchell

New Harbor Press

Rapid City, SD

New Harbor Press
1601 Mt Rushmore Rd, Ste 3288
Rapid City, SD 57701
www.newharborpress.com

Ordering Information:
Quantity sales. Special discounts are available on quantity purchases by corporations, associations, and others. For details, contact the "Special Sales Department" at the address above.

Grace, Love, and Some Football/Mitchell —1st ed.

ISBN 978-1-63357-476-2

First edition: 10 9 8 7 6 5 4 3 2 1

Introduction

Once, in a small town rich in history, there lived an old, simple married couple. They didn't have much, but they had each other—and their God. Each day, they would sit outside on their front porch and enjoy the arousing aroma of burgers grilling over charcoal. The pleasure of a cigarette puff and a sip of cold beer was unmistakable. These two were simple—yet filled with pure love and simple pleasures. There was a mysterious and inviting quality about them. Their lives seemed uncomplicated, but their hearts overflowed with joy and contentment. They welcomed anyone and everyone to join them for burgers and conversation. If you lingered, you were invited to their firepit; free to sing, dance, and be silly along with them. Whenever you saw this couple, you felt seen—not just superficially but truly seen. There was genuine love and care in every interaction. They shared their hardships and listened to yours, offering encouragement. You'd never feel even a hint of judgment. Their wisdom, heartfelt and genuine, was always freely offered.

If you ever get a chance to stop by this humble home, you can rest assured that you will be made to feel at home with a juicy burger, a cold drink, a warm fire, and a genuine conversation.

One day, when I was blessed to be in their lovely company, I wanted to ask them how they had stayed so madly in love with each other, and I wanted to hear their story. Of course, the old man sat me down while he was at the grill, and he asked me, "So you want to hear our story, huh? Well, I would say, it all started with some Grace, Love, and some Football."

This is their story . . . .

Contents

PART 1

High School Years

CHAPTER 1

Jonathan Steele

Jonathan Steele grew up in a wealthy family in a wealthy home in a small town in Texas—a town where everyone knew everyone. The town's culture was highly sports-oriented, and anyone who was anyone was involved in sports in some capacity. Jonathan aspired to be the best quarterback that this town has ever known. His father was the starting quarterback in his day, and his grandfather, and his great-grandfather; greatness was in his blood.

His father was the owner of the biggest and most successful company in his town. The company was called "Steele Manufacturing," and it was the lifeblood of this community. The company was the lead manufacturer of steel used to produce military weapons throughout the state of Texas. Steele Manufacturing was founded by Jonathan's father. As the only child of his parents, Jonathan was expected to inherit the family business after completing his college education and earning his master's degree in business.

Even though his life was pretty well set up for him, there was tension between Jonathan and his father. Jonathan always strived to do his best and be good enough for his father, but his best felt like it was never good enough. When it came to working out for the school football team, his father would make him run drills every day until dusk. And after his workout, he was to go to his room and study for school, as well as read books on running a business. If and when Jonathan would complain or not meet his father's standards, he would get a beating with a belt in the backyard. Oftentimes, those beatings happened when his father was drunk. His mother hated seeing how Jonathan was treated, but she knew her place and could not speak out against her husband.

His parents, if he could even try to imagine it, used to be the fun couple of the town, hosting parties and organizing all social gatherings. His father was the starting quarterback at the local high school and went on to be the starting quarterback at a prominent university in Texas. His mother was also raised in a wealthy family. She was the prom queen, and all the guys in school wanted her, while the girls wanted to be like her. But after they got married and after his mother had a miscarriage of a baby boy that happened before he was born, everything changed. His father became bitter, and his mother became destroyed by grief and guilt. Now, his mother is essentially existing to try to please his father, and his father, when he is not at Steele Manufacturing, is either at the local bar or at home drinking bottles of whiskey.

Only when Jonathan was at school could he feel like he could actually breathe. Everybody at his high school respected him and wanted to be around him. The guys wanted to be him, and the girls wanted to be with him. It was his paradise. School was easy for him because his father had always made him read academic books to prepare for his journey to earn his master's degree in business, so that he could take over Steele Manufacturing. And on that practice field at football practice, he could truly come alive. He could outrun every single person on that field and throw the football with so much precision that he could be in the NFL, throwing among the all-stars. His main friends were the team's starting running back, Tommy, and the two starting wide receivers, Bobby and Jeffrey. Everyone at their high school and amongst all the football teams knew them as the "Quadruple Threat." On and off the field, the Quadruple Threat was unstoppable. No group of guys could be more stunning and likable off the field, yet so savage and determined on the field. No one knew the potential of the Quadruple Threat more than the football team's coach, Coach Joe. Coach Joe was the most respected football coach you could ever meet, and he led the team to many victories over the twenty years he coached. Coach Joe lived, breathed, and even bled football. It was his greatest passion and sole goal in life. If he wasn't coaching football, he was watching tapes or sleeping and dreaming of his next game. If Coach Joe knew that a player had potential, you were automatically his best friend, and he would stick his neck out for you with anything that you might need. But for a majority of players, he was your worst nightmare. Coach Joe would drill you worse than a United States Marine Drill Sergeant. If you make a mistake, it is the last mistake that you will ever make, unless you are a glutton for punishment and enjoy up-downs until you pass out or run marathons all night long. You keep your eyes on that ball, and you hold on to that ball with your life. If you fumble that football, it might as well be the last thing you ever do.

With all of the intensity that goes on with the football team, there was one thing that could lighten the mood for the entire team. There is a scrawny sophomore kid named Jimmy whose dream is to play on the football team as a running back. No one on the team takes Jimmy seriously, not even Coach Joe, who has a hard time putting up with him. As a coach who can't refuse to have anyone on a team, Coach Joe has him do all the inconvenient tasks that no one really wants to do, such as setting up the practice field, cleaning up after practice, being the waterboy at games, and generally doing little tasks to make him feel "needed." Oftentimes, as Jimmy would set up the practice field, the team would pick on him, pushing him down while carrying things from the team shed to the field, and call him names like, "Hey, what's up, Scrawny J, how's the running back dream coming along?" No one had more fun picking on Jimmy than Jonathan and the Quadruple Threat. Picking on Jimmy really, in a messed-up way, internally made Jonathan release all of the anger, self-hatred, depression, family trauma, and unmet expectations onto Jimmy. It was almost like an addictive drug, the release it gave Jonathan, putting all of his inner turmoil onto Jimmy. And because of how well-respected Jonathan was throughout the team, almost everyone went along with Jonathan, especially the guys who comprise the Quadruple Threat, Tommy, Bobby, and Jeffrey. Often, after Jimmy had set up the game field, Jonathan and the gang would go to everything that Jimmy set up and either tossed the items on the ground or threw them out of place so that when Coach Joe would come to the field, Jimmy would get verbally reamed by Coach Joe and then have him run a few miles and set up the field again.

Coach Joe would even give in to saying *"Scrawny J "* and pointing out how far he is from ever having an opportunity to step on the field as a running back. The most traumatic thing that happened to Jimmy occurred one Monday morning after Jonathan had a tough weekend with his father. On the previous Friday night, the football team lost its game due to an interception that Jonathan threw on the last play of the game. That interception that Jonathan threw led to a *pick-six;* in other words, the interception led to the opposing team's defensive player running for a touchdown. When Jonathan came home from that game, his father got home a couple of hours later from the bar, completely drunk. His father came home, went for a bottle of whiskey, and then downed the bottle, throwing the bottle at Jonathan, throwing him up against the wall, jabbing him in his stomach, throwing him in the backyard, taking his belt off, and giving him a brutal whipping before locking him out of the house that night. So, on that Monday, Jonathan went up to Jimmy, having Tommy, Bobby, and Jeffrey hold him against the team shed, punching him repeatedly in the stomach and locking him in the shed. When Coach Joe found out about this, he apologized to Jimmy and gave him a week off from practices. Coach Joe informed Jonathan and the Quadruple Threat that he had to punish them with an after-school detention, explaining that the behavior they had exhibited was unacceptable. With the extent of how they treated Jimmy, they knew that they were getting away with a slap on the wrist, and they did decide that they would never do that again, but in a messed-up way, Jonathan still believed that he needed that release after the abuse that he received from his own father that previous Friday night.

Besides the fulfilling feeling of playing football, the only other saving grace of Jonathan's life was Lisa Smith. Even though everyone throughout the entire high school acted like they were all about Jonathan, he knew that was just because of his status and abilities. Jonathan knew that he could "get with" any girl in his high school, but Lisa was different. Lisa saw Jonathan for who he really was. She wouldn't put up with his crap and would criticize him when he deserved it. Lisa also genuinely asked him how he was really doing every day, not just the fake, "Hey, what's up? How are you?" Instead, it felt like she could stare inside his soul. She could sense when he was hurting, when he needed someone to talk to, when he just needed to laugh, or if he needed to cry. Jonathan never met anyone in his entire life who actually saw him, the real him. Lisa wasn't the most attractive girl in the school, but she was bold and genuinely wanted to make a difference in the school. She was on the student board fighting against bullying, racism, sexism, and intolerance in any way. She usually had no interest in athletes, especially male athletes, because of how cocky, arrogant, and self-centered they often were, but with

Jonathan, it was a different story. It's like the universe drew them to each other.

After the terrible incident involving Jimmy, instead of yelling at Jonathan with a lecture and judgment, she knew what to ask him: "What's going on at home?" Jonathan knew that he couldn't hide the fact from her that his dad severely abused him after losing that Friday night game. He confessed to her that taking his anger, aggression, hurt, and self-hatred and releasing it onto Jimmy was the only way that he could feel sane and find a sense of relief. Lisa appreciated that he confessed that to her and genuinely wanted to help him. She made sure to be clear with him that she wanted to help Jonathan in any way possible. Lisa would always be a shoulder to cry on, a listening ear, and someone he could always trust, but she would not approve of his mistreatment of anyone, especially Jimmy. Jonathan knew that he could not lose what he had in Lisa, and he agreed that he shouldn't justify his mistreatment of Jimmy because of his own abuse from his father.

As the football season was coming to an end, Jonathan and his team were making it to the championship game! Everyone in the school was so ecstatic. If the football team wasn't already school celebrities, they were once the news came out that they were going to the championship.

The senior class invited the entire football team to a celebration party at one of the typical house party spots to celebrate their huge accomplishment of making it to the championship game! The guests of honor would be the "Quadruple Threat"—Jonathan at quarterback, Tommy at running back, and Jeffrey and Bobby, the wide receivers. Everyone who was anyone would be at this party. Of course, Jonathan wanted Lisa to be his guest of honor at the party, but she never felt comfortable at such events. She felt like they were always full of egotistical and self-centered preps and jocks. The fact that Lisa didn't enjoy hanging out with his people always kind of got on his nerves, but he understood and respected her decision.

So that Saturday night, which was the weekend before the big championship game, Jonathan picked up his bros in his father's Corvette so that the Quadruple Threat would show up to this party in style. When they arrived at the party, everyone was cheering and chanting, *"Never forget the Quadruple Threat!"* They could barely step out of the Corvette, and everyone was trying to hand them a beer, asking, "Are you guys ready to destroy the Florida Gators?!" Tommy, the running back, shouted, "See ya later, Gators, the Texas Rangers aren't gonna show you any favors as we arise as saviors!" With that shout, everyone screamed and cheered. As the night progressed, Jonathan and the gang played beer pong with anyone who wanted to challenge them, and then, after a while, it evolved into taking shots around the bonfire. Jonathan and the Quadruple Threat were having the time of their lives, that was until Jonathan received a text from his mother. His mother sent him a text saying, *"I think you should head home, your father was walking home from the bar and was hit by a truck. He didn't make it."* Jonathan was drunk and devastated. The drinking finally ended his old man, and he didn't know what to think. He was angry, he was heartbroken, all of his emotions were going crazy and were exaggerated by the amount he drank. He gathered up Tommy, Jeffrey, and Bobby and said that they needed to drive. The Quadruple Threat gathered into the Corvette, and Jonathan revved his engine and went 0 to 60 miles per hour in a matter of seconds on the gravel road outside the party house. His reckless driving really freaked out the guys. Jonathan then made a sharp left turn into the main city street, ignoring the stop sign, and they were T-boned by a pickup truck. Jonathan and Bobby were in the front, and the airbags went off, saving their lives, but they were really beat up. Tommy and Jeffrey were in the back seat and were thrown out of the car; they didn't make it.

The police arrived at the scene. The pickup driver was alright, but very concerned because he knew these boys and knew that they were on the high school football team. The police were able to rescue Jonathan and Bobby. Even though they seemed to be alright, they did have the ambulance take them to the local hospital. When Jonathan was put into a hospital bed, he freaked out and screamed, saying that he needed to be home with his mom. But they just said they need to have him rest and recover. Jonathan wished to himself that he had been the one who died. He now had to face his mother, who had just lost her husband to a drunken car accident, and now her son got himself into a drunken car accident. He knew that he didn't deserve forgiveness.

Jimmy (Scrawny J)

Jimmy was on his long Saturday morning run on the local gravel road. After a long and trying football season, his team finally reached the championship game. With all his heart, he wanted to play at least one game as a running back. He remembered watching the Dallas Cowboys with his dad when he was younger, before his dad passed away. They would always cheer for the Cowboys on Sundays after church. His dad was a running back when he was in high school, and Jimmy admired that and strived to walk in his father's footsteps. His dad passed away from cancer when he was in the fifth grade, and it devastated him. Now his mom had to get a job after being a stay-at-home mom. She had to work two jobs. She worked as a janitor at Steele Manufacturing and then worked at the local bar in the evenings. Jimmy could see the pain in her eyes from the long hours that she put into her work. She couldn't even put supper on the table for them. Due to their situation, Jimmy was eligible for the free and reduced lunch program at school. He hated to be seen as poor, and the bullies in his high school didn't let him forget it. His only outlet was his love of running. When all the pain and dark thoughts started arising in his mind, they could all be released as he would run for miles and miles. With every step, he would dream of making his father proud and becoming the starting running back on his high school football team. Jimmy knew what people thought of him. A skinny, scrawny, poor kid who had no future. His coach, Coach Joe, was the person he looked up to most, even though the respect wasn't mutual. All of his fellow football teammates called him "Scrawny J." He was prepared for that from his fellow teammates, but when Coach Joe called him that horrible name, it killed him inside. Every minute of football practice, Jimmy tried to prove his worth. He got to practice early to set up the field for practice. He was the waterboy for the team's starters. He would also clean up the field after practice. With everything he did for the football team, he hoped and prayed that Coach Joe would acknowledge his hard work and ambition, and at the very least, give him a chance. But instead, along with the team, Coach Joe would go along with his stupid and demeaning nickname, *"Scrawny J."*

On the previous Monday, the last week of practice before the championship game, the most popular and well-liked football player of the entire high school, Quarterback Jonathan Steele, alongside the most arrogant and preppy people he had ever known, the Quadruple Threat, came to the football field early. Led by Jonathan, the Quadruple Threat, they held him up against the shed where all the football equipment was stored, and Jonathan punched him repeatedly, and then they threw him into the shed and locked it for Coach Joe to find him. This was the first time that Coach Joe actually acknowledged that he was being mistreated. Even though all the pain and the disrespect he experienced were humiliating, Jimmy finally felt seen by the coach. He finally felt hopeful that this experience would help Coach Joe remember how much he does for the team and consider him to at least share in the running back position. If only Coach Joe would allow him to run drills during practice and see how much work Jimmy has put into running. Yes, he wasn't the strongest or most muscular guy on the team, but Jimmy knew he was fast and had endurance. Jimmy knew the team's playbook like the back of his hand. He would often run the drills in his dreams at night.

After Jimmy's Saturday morning run, he went home to try to find something to eat before he started his homework for the weekend. Even though they didn't have much to eat at home, his mom always made sure to leave a frozen pizza in the freezer. He definitely loved pizza, and he could never say no to a pizza. After he ate and finished his homework, he turned on the TV, got himself a pop, and some popcorn, and then turned on his favorite show in the world, *The Twilight Zone*. He often wished he could be in the Twilight Zone and wake up to be the best running back in the NFL. He also loved the old-school shock and awe of *The Twilight Zone*. Jimmy was very health-conscious, but on Saturday nights when he was home alone while his mom was at work, it was Twilight Zone night for him, and he would veg out with a pop and popcorn. He actually really enjoyed these Twilight Zone nights. But on this Twilight Zone night, he got an unexpected phone call from his mom.

Apparently, two significant events occurred this Saturday night. His mom's boss at Steele Manufacturing, Frank Steele, was at the local bar where she worked on evenings and weekends, where he usually was, and he ended up getting way too drunk (like usual). Still, on this particular night, he ended up walking home and was hit by a truck and died. On top of that, after the big high school party for the school's football team, which of course he wasn't invited to, Jonathan and the Quadruple Threat were driving in a Corvette, leaving the party, and they were hit by a pickup truck. The police released the information that Running Back Tommy Johnson and Wide Receiver Jeffrey Thomson were killed on the scene as they were thrown out of the Corvette. Quarterback Jonathan Steele and Wide Receiver Bobby Holt did survive and were alright. Jimmy didn't know what to think about all of this. Of course, Jimmy knew that this was a massive loss to the community and that it was really sad to have all this tragedy. He hated to think like this, but he couldn't help but think that the Quadruple Threat was such an essential asset to the school's football team, and he feared that this news could really affect the championship game. Tommy Johnson was an incredible running back, but he definitely did not treat Jimmy fairly, and Tommy played every play as a running back in the football games. No one ever considered giving Jimmy a shot at playing running back. Was this his shot at being a running back? During the championship game?

Chapter 3

Lisa Smith

Lisa Smith, being a black girl in high school, felt like she was expected to be interested in all things sports. Her twin brother, who lives with her father in Oklahoma, was all about basketball. Her dad was in the NBA and hooked up with her mom back in college, and then left her for the NBA. Lisa's brother did everything to live in their father's footsteps. Leaving Lisa and their mom on their own, she wanted nothing to do with sports. Lisa instead wanted to be known for pursuing a career as a social justice warrior. She was in the student council fighting against bullying, racism, sexism, and intolerance in any way. Her dream was to attend college and pursue a career in counseling.

Despite her total disdain for sports, there was one person who would bring her back to the world of sports. His name was Jonathan Steele. Usually, everything about Jonathan would be a red flag in her book. He was the most popular guy in school, starting as quarterback on the school's football team, and was the son of the owner of the most corporate and soul-sucking company in their town, Steele Manufacturing. Steele Manufacturing was the primary manufacturer of steel used to produce military weapons throughout Texas. The company made the town's wealthy individuals even wealthier, and everyone else was essentially forced to work there, as it was one of the few companies in town to offer employment opportunities. It was fair to say that 75 percent of the community worked for Steele Manufacturing, and if you weren't high up in the company, you busted your butt in that warehouse for twelve long hours a day assembling the steel parts for military weapons.

Lisa's mom was employed there, and every day it seemed to drain the life and joy out of her completely. The company did not care about their well-being. They had to produce a massive amount of product with only three breaks in the workday. Lisa hated that her mom had to work for a company that encouraged warmongering and the alt-right political agenda—corporate greed at its finest. Conservatives always seemed to say they were for the "working man," but it sure felt like they just cared about putting more money in rich people's pockets. Despite all of that, there was still something about this Jonathan Steele. Something she could never put into words, but there was something different about him. Lisa believed that deep inside of Jonathan, he had a loving soul that was corrupted by the abuse of his father. She knows that the effects of the abuse ran deep, and he often took it out in unhealthy and unhelpful ways. There was just an incident that reflected this. There was this poor student in school named Jimmy, who was on the football team, whom Jonathan picked on. His bullying escalated significantly after Jonathan felt that he was the reason the football team lost an important game. Jonathan punched Jimmy and locked him in the football storage shed. This behavior really upset Lisa because she is such an advocate for social justice and anti-bullying. But Lisa knew there was a deeper story. Jonathan's father severely took out his anger on Jonathan, and Jonathan saw this behavior as a release from his pain. Lisa hoped to help Jonathan with better coping skills.

Lisa was beyond excited to spend time with Jonathan after this football season. Jonathan just recently asked her to be his date to the prom. She didn't get to experience prom during their junior year, and she really wanted to. Despite all his "tough guy" persona, Lisa knew that Jonathan was a softy at heart. She knew he was deeply in love with her, and she knew she was just as deeply in love with him. They would be dressed to the nines, and they were highly probable to be this year's Prom King and Queen. Even though Lisa wasn't the "prettiest" girl in school, she was highly respected for her fight for social change, and that really made her feel like she was making a difference. Of course, Jonathan was likely to be Prom King because he is the most popular guy at school; he was pretty much the school celebrity. The leader of the "Quadruple Threat" is also the leader of the football team. Even though she didn't believe in the pretentious popularity contest of high school life, she did feel pretty special that she had a special place in Jonathan's heart. It made her heart tingle inside. Also, this summer, they have a bunch of plans to do their favorite pastime - camping and having drinks around the firepit. Lisa did not like drinking in public events, but she did enjoy sneaking drinks with Jonathan. They would bring a stolen 12-pack of beer and a pack of cigarettes from Jonathan's father's hidden stash. They would have some drinks, smoke a few cigarettes, and talk long into the night about their dreams, their beliefs, their deepest and darkest secrets, their highs and lows, and everything in between. He never pressured her to be intimate, which she really respected. It was just about spending quality time together. Thinking about camping with Jonathan always gave her goosebumps. It was naughty, but not too naughty, and it was just a wonderful experience. Lisa knew that Jonathan would one day be her husband. They just needed to get out of this petty time of their lives called high school. Because when it was just Jonathan and her, it was a dream come true.

With the big championship game coming up, Jonathan and the Quadruple Threat were going to be the stars at the big celebration party before the big game. Lisa knew that Jonathan had to go, and he asked her to be his guest of honor. As flattering as the invite was, she just couldn't bring herself to want to go to such a pretentious high school party with a bunch of preppy and drunk idiots. She would instead read the book that she was working on. She knew that disappointed Jonathan, but she also appreciated that he understood and respected her decision.

After Lisa cuddled up on the couch with a blanket and a warm mug of hot chocolate topped with whipped cream, she began reading her book about racial injustice and the fight for racial freedom. This was her favorite type of book to read. Although as she was reading, she couldn't help but have this weird thought that something bad was going to happen. She wasn't worried that Jonathan would sleep around on her, because she knew that both of them wanted to wait until marriage, and they held to their convictions. But still something felt off. She couldn't help but send him a text asking if he was alright. Right as she sent that text, Lisa received a text from her friend that read, *"Jonathan got in a drunk driving accident."* She gasped in shock. What could she do?

CHAPTER 4

Coach Joe

Coach Joe lived and breathed football. Football is his everything. He sacrificed relationships, vacations, and sleep. He sacrificed so much because all his mind wanted to think about was football. Thinking about how to get that next touchdown was almost like an addiction. Coach Joe coached the same high school football team that he played quarterback for when he was in high school. The good ol' Texas Rangers football ran through his veins. He coached this team for twenty years, and he finally had the perfect team. He had the "Quadruple Threat" consisting of Jonathan Steele at quarterback, Tommy Johnson at running back, and Jeffrey Thomson and Bobby Holt, the wide receivers. They were the most talented and most dedicated players he had ever had the opportunity to coach. And out of all the talent of the Quadruple Threat, he really had his eye on Jonathan Steele. Jonathan reminded him of himself back in his heyday. Coach Joe could just see it in Jonathan's eyes. The hunger, the thirst, the need to win. He didn't just play to win; he played to survive and thrive. When the rest of the team ran one mile, Jonathan would run two. When practice was at 6:00 a.m., Jonathan was there at 5:00 a.m. If he ever made a mistake, he would run that play until he dropped dead and then get up and do it one more time. True dedication.

Coach Joe didn't just love football; he lived football. He will never forget the last game he ever played. It was the NCAA College Football Championship. He was the starting quarterback for the Texas Longhorns playing against the Oklahoma Sooners. The NFL Scouts were all at that game. Coach Joe had always wanted to play for the Dallas Cowboys, and a scout from the team was in attendance at that game. The pressure was on, and Coach Joe thrived under pressure. Nothing could have gotten in his way, until something did. It was the final play, and he was about to throw the game-winning pass to a wide receiver, but then the defensive line rushed the line of scrimmage, sacking him, twisting his knee, and breaking every bone in it. Coach Joe was carted off the field during that game, and his opportunity to play for the Dallas Cowboys ended that day, marking the end of his football career. That was the most heartbreaking day in his entire life. That day pretty much killed him inside. But thankfully, after a couple of years of recovery, Coach Joe was hired on as the football coach at his high school, the Texas Rangers. Coach Joe's mission with coaching has always been to help someone become who they have always wanted to be, playing in the NFL. He would coach that player to be the best player that he could be. His biggest fear was letting that player suffer the same injury he had, which would end the player's football career. Jonathan was the perfect player for fulfilling his coaching dream. He had everything to be the best.

There was this one kid who really got on Coach Joe's nerves. His name was Jimmy, but everyone called him *Scrawny J,* a fitting nickname for his slender build. One thing that really got onto Coach Joe's nerves, which was probably due to jealousy, was that Jimmy's father had played for the Dallas Cowboys, and now this kid, Jimmy, thought he would do the same. This kid was too skinny and lacked the build to be great. Admittedly, Coach Joe did not give him the time of day. To get Jimmy off his back, he thought he would let Jimmy feel useful by having him set up the practice field and be the waterboy at games, because there was no chance Coach Joe would be willing to risk losing a game by letting this Scrawny J play at running back. Not when he had the Quadruple Threat that dominated every game.

This fantastic football season was coming to an end. However, in the last game of the regular season, Jonathan ended up throwing an interception that ultimately cost them the game. To many, it wasn't the end of the world because they still had a good enough record to get into the playoffs, but to Coach Joe, it was a punch in the gut. Giving up these big moments is detrimental to the player, and this wasn't just any player; this was Jonathan Steele. Coach Joe put so many hours into coaching Jonathan, and to see that kind of error was unacceptable. These kinds of mistakes can ruin your career. So, after the game, Coach Joe made Jonathan run five miles on the field while everyone else had left. Jonathan didn't question it because he knew those kinds of mistakes were unacceptable. Coach Joe knew that the next week of practice would be intense because the team needed to focus on winning their next game to avoid missing the opportunity to play in the championship game.

On the following Monday, as Coach Joe was getting on the field for practice, he heard some banging and screaming coming from the storage shed. Finding out that the Quadruple Threat beat on Jimmy and locked him in the shed, Coach Joe was furious. Why the hell would they do this? Coach Joe sincerely apologized to Jimmy and gave him a free week off from his duties at practice. He did make Jonathan, Tommy, Jeffrey, and Bobby run two miles before practice started and gave them a week of after-school de-tention. Coach Joe knew that he couldn't punish them too much because of the importance of this time in the season. Still, it gave him a motive to make these last weeks of practice hell for them, because Coach Joe was not going to let stupidity be the reason they didn't make it to this championship game, after all the progress they had made this season.

The playoffs were going well after Coach Joe really drilled into the team and in no way let them have any slack. They were winning games and building back their confidence. Everyone in school was very excited, and Principal Clark was impressed with his coaching. He offered Coach Joe that if he got the team the championship, Principal Clark would bump up his salary by 20 percent. That was huge! So, when the final victory came in the last game of the playoffs, Coach Joe became even more excited.

It was the weekend before the championship game, and Coach Joe felt like he deserved to let off some steam from all the tension that he had been under this season, so he decided to go to the local bar for a nice cold beer that Saturday night. To his surprise, he saw Jonathan's father at the bar. Coach Joe figured he would come up and say hi to his dad after he had had a couple of beers. Coach Joe figured he would really respect Jonathan's father because he raised a hardworking and talented son, but to his surprise, Jonathan's dad seemed like a really crappy person. He was toasted and arguing with anyone he could, and he was actually bad-mouthing Jonathan to everyone in the bar. After a while, Coach Joe got irritated enough to decide to confront Jonathan's dad and said, "You know your son is the best athlete I've had in my football program in twenty years. I think you have had enough to drink and should head home." That really agitated Jonathan's father, and in his drunkenness, he attempted to punch Coach Joe. After the bartender saw this, he went to Jonathan's father and told him that he needed to leave. Coach Joe thanked the bartender. Then the bartender started small talk with Coach Joe, congratulating him on the great football season. Then, about a half hour later, the bartender received a call that Jonathan's father had died after getting hit by a truck at an intersection. Then the next thing you know, there was another call about a car accident involving four high school kids in a Corvette that was hit by a truck. They learned that the high school kids were the boys in the group called "The Quadruple Threat." They realized that Jonathan Steele and Bobby Holt were in the front seats of the Corvette and survived but were really beaten up. They also learned that Tommy Johnson and Jeffrey Thomson were in the back seat of the Corvette, and they were thrown out of the vehicle, and they did not survive. When Coach Joe saw this, he fell to his knees in hysterics. He was devastated. Not them, not the Quadruple Threat! They were the best players he had ever coached. And the championship is under a week away! There is no way! How could a good God allow such cruelty?! If he ever believed in a god, this was his final straw. There was no way a good God would ever allow this much suffering and death.

CHAPTER 5

The Championship Game

It was the night of the big game. Tensions were high. The community was in mourning over the losses that had occurred the previous weekend, and Coach Joe knew that the community needed this win to honor the memories of the deceased. Not only did the community lose the owner of the leading business and employer of the community, Frank Steele of Steele Manufacturing, but they also lost two kids from the local high school and star players of the football team, Tommy Johnson and Jeffrey Thomson, as well as two other students suffering injuries, Jonathan Steele and Bobby Holt. Coach Joe knew as well how important this win was for his career. Principal Clark told Coach Joe that if they won this year's championship game, he would get a 20 percent increase in his salary. So, the pressure was definitely high for this championship game. Everyone in the community was in the stands at the football stadium, all with the hopes that they could win this game in honor of Tommy Johnson and Jeffrey Thomson. It might sound silly, but this win could really help with the healing process of this community.

With all of the intensity building, the opposing team, the Florida Gators, came out on the field, and they looked twice the size of their team, the Texas Rangers. The Florida Gators were full of intensity and just as loud. Still, thankfully, the quarterback, Jonathan Steele, was just as motivated and was becoming pumped with hearing the crowd do the Texas Rangers chant: *"See ya later Gators, the Texas Rangers aren't gonna show you any favors as we arise as saviors!"*

Even though Jonathan was injured in the accident, along with Wide Receiver Bobby Holt, they were still filled with passion and aggression. They were driven by inner resentment and the hurt of losing their best friends, Tommy and Jeffrey, of the Quadruple Threat. Not only did Jonathan lose half of the Quadruple Threat, but he also lost his father. Jonathan's relationship was very complicated and unhealthy, but he still held a great deal of respect for his dad and had a deep-seated need to make his father proud. Frank Steele was not only a very successful and well-known quarterback in his community, but he also started and ran the most successful business that employed a majority of the community. Jonathan felt like he had huge shoes to fill.

Coach Joe sent out his two star players, the remaining members of the former Quadruple Threat, Quarterback Jonathan Steele and Wide Receiver Bobby Holt, to the coin toss as the crowd was cheering on their team, the Texas Rangers. The excitement as well as the stress were at the top of the scale. Coach Joe thrived under stress; he knew that he just had to coach like he always did and lean into his love for the game. He knew that Jonathan was no stranger to stress and hard work. Coach Joe believed in his team, and he wouldn't let them, his school, or his community down. He has been coaching this team for twenty years, and this was by far the best and most qualified team he has ever led to a championship game win. The opposing team, the Florida Gators, won the coin toss and chose to receive the ball first. Coach Joe knew that they wanted to intimidate the Texas Rangers and start strong. Their intensity was powerful and made very clear.

After the kickoff, Coach Joe sent his defense onto the field. The Texas Rangers have the best defense in the league, and they came to play. The defense knew that they might have to be the strength of the team to win this game, considering they had only half of the Quadruple Threat, and the remaining two, Jonathan and Bobby, were injured on top of it.

The Gators' quarterback got to the line, and the game started. . While the Rangers' defense gave it their all, stopping the Gators' run game at the line of scrimmage, the Gators' were still able to be successful with their passing game. First down after first down, the Gators were inching their way to the goal line. When they reached the red zone, twenty yards from the goal line, the Rangers' defense finally stopped the passes in the in-zone, and the Gators were forced to attempt a field goal. After they successfully kicked the field goal, everyone on the Texas Rangers' sideline and the defense, even though they had stopped the Gators from scoring a touchdown, knew now that they were going to have to come from behind, and the nerves and seriousness of the game really hit everyone. This was going to be the most challenging game of their season by far.

Jonathan came up to the line of scrimmage, looking into the eyes of the defensive line, trying to pretend that he wasn't intimidated. Jonathan shouted, "Down, set, hut," and grabbed the ball, retreating behind the offensive line, hoping to God that he would find Wide Receiver Bobby open to catch the ball. The Gators' defense was not about to let their star receiver open, so that forced Jonathan to look for other open receivers. Once he found the tight end open, Jonathan threw the ball, but the defensive player had his eye on the ball, and right off the bat, Jonathan's throw was intercepted.

As the game progressed, the Rangers' defense was doing its best but was becoming exhausted. Fortunately, they were able to contain the Gators' passing game, and besides one touchdown, they were limited to field goals.

Every time Jonathan came back on the field, he knew that he could not throw any more interceptions or they were going to lose this game, so he leaned really heavily into handing the ball off to the second-string running back. Unfortunately, at best, the running back was making it a yard or two. More often than not, the running back wouldn't make it past the line of scrimmage, and after three plays, the Rangers continually had to kick off the ball. They haven't even scored a first down yet. The game was getting even more intimidating and nerve-racking. Thankfully, due to the defense, they were not yet totally out of the game, and if they could figure something out in the second half, the Rangers may stand a chance. Jonathan knew that Coach Joe could rally the guys at halftime and get their momentum going. At halftime, the score was *Florida Gators 19, Texas Rangers 0.*

Throughout the entire first half, through all the stress, Coach Joe was continually getting harassed by Scrawny J to get a chance to run a play at running back. That was the last thing that Coach Joe wanted to deal with. He is actually trying to win this game, and the last thing that he thought could ever help anything was this scrawny Jimmy trying to run the ball. If anything, he would end up with a player who needed to get med-carted off the field.

After halftime, there was a renewed energy on the team and the offense was ready to hit the field. Jonathan and Bobby were determined to pull off an outstanding offensive play. Jonathan went up to the line of scrimmage, staring the defensive lineman across from him dead in the eyes, shouting, "Down, set, hut" with the most intensity he had shown throughout the whole game. Bobby jolted off the line of scrimmage once Jonathan shouted hut and ran his route. He ran full speed at the defensive player who was guarding him and then spun to his right, jolting to his left to get open. Bobby was open for the catch midfield, and Jonathan saw him. Right when Jonathan brought his arm back to throw the ball, the defensive lineman he was staring at saw Jonathan's eyes and lifted his arms at the right moment, grabbing the ball midair and catching it, then running it all the way for the touchdown, giving him the pick-six. Coach Joe and everyone in the stands were silent, and their heads, which had been held high for the second half, all sank as their hopes for winning this championship game faded. After the Gators kicked their extra point, the score was *Florida Gators 26, Texas Rangers 0.*

It was time for the Rangers to receive the ball again, but the motivation just wasn't there anymore. The receiver caught the ball at the 26-yard line and was brought down right away. The guy who brought the receiver down got up and spat at the receiver, saying, "So much for the best team in the league, haha."

After Jimmy saw the total look of defeat in Coach Joe's eyes, he went up to ask one more time, saying, "Come on, Coach, what do you have to lose?" And Coach Joe hesitantly agreed and left him with saying this, "Just don't get your scrawny ass killed, okay?" Jimmy nodded and went out to the offensive huddle, totally excited, and gave Jonathan the play as instructed by the coach. Jonathan, in total shock, said, "Okay, if that's what Coach Joe said, we'll give it a try."

Jimmy lined up at the running back position behind Jonathan and noticed the defensive lineman who had just intercepted

Jonathan's last throw, and the defensive lineman couldn't help but bust out laughing. The whole offense couldn't help but feel embarrassed while hearing everyone laughing at Scrawny J and all shouting, "We're gonna kill that kid just for fun." Everyone on that defensive line started staring at Jimmy to intimidate him. All the intimidation just hyped up Jimmy all the more.

"Down, set, hut," Jonathan shouted as he grabbed the football and started traveling backwards to hand off the football to Scrawny J. Jimmy grabbed that football and with everything in him began to run, going in and out of the defensive players and running past every single defensive player, and ran faster than anyone had ever seen on that football field. After Jimmy got past everyone, both teams just stopped in their tracks and watched him cross the goal line. Jimmy scored the first touchdown for the team, running 74 yards. The whole world seemed to stop in place for a moment. No one believed what they had just witnessed. Then everyone in the arena cheered at the top of their lungs. Players from both teams rushed to congratulate him. Coach Joe, after falling to his knees in utter shock, couldn't do anything but thank God and repent for the way he treated Jimmy. Coach Joe ran up to Jimmy and stopped to say, "I have seen a lot of football in my day. I have won a lot of football. I have seen many upsets in my day, but I have never witnessed anything like what I just saw. I always questioned my belief in whether there is a God. After we lost Tommy Johnson, Jeffrey Thomson, and Frank Steele, I totally gave up trying to believe in God. There was no way that a good God would ever allow what happened on that dreaded night. But then, tonight happened, and you went and outran everyone on this field and ran faster than anyone I have ever seen. All I can do is ask God for His forgiveness and ask you for yours. Son, you are one hell of a football player. Will you please forgive me?" Coach Joe and Jimmy hugged, and Jimmy smiled the biggest smile of his whole life.

The score is now *Florida Gators 26, Texas Rangers 7*. It was time for the Rangers to kick the football to the Gators. The whole crowd had a brand new energy. The Rangers had a refreshed energy. When the defense came out on the field, they stopped every play that the Gators ran. After three and out, the Gators kicked off the ball to the Rangers, and it was time for them to come back out on offense, with Jimmy coming out as the starting running back. Jonathan couldn't help but give Jimmy a side hug and said, "You can call the shots from now on, Jimmy." This was the first time Jimmy ever heard Jonathan not address him as Scrawny J, and he couldn't help but smile.

Play after play, Jimmy felt increasingly alive. The crowd was all cheering him on, chanting, *"Go, Jimmy, Go!"* The confidence returned for the entire team. Jonathan was finally able to complete some passes to Bobby, allowing the offense to mix up the types of plays to keep the defense off balance. For the remainder of the game, the Rangers scored touchdowns on every drive. Jimmy ended up scoring two more touchdowns, and Bobby was able to catch a pass in the in-zone, making the final score of the game *Texas Rangers 28, Florida Gators 26.*

When the game clock went to zero, everyone ran up to Jimmy to congratulate him. Jonathan lifted Jimmy onto his shoulders, and everyone cheered and chanted his name!

After the game, the team gathered in the locker room, and Coach Joe grabbed a football and had the team sit down, all except for Jimmy. To the whole team, Coach Joe started saying, "I have seen a lot of football in my day. I love football. The game of football flows through my veins. When I wake up, my day is centered around football, and when I sleep, my dreams are of football. I have never seen better football than I have saw from this young man standing with me now. Every football practice and every football game, in my mind, I was agitated by this Scrawny J, always feeling harassed by the number of times he asked me to give him a chance. Time and time again, I shoved him off and had him do the grunt work of the team to make him feel important and get him off my back. I believe that how I treated Jimmy is a reflection of how I treated and what I thought about God. I felt agitated and even harassed when anyone would bring up my need for God in my life. What could a far and distant God do for me? I felt like I had everything under control. Then, as you know, as a team, as a school, as a community, everything got turned upside down when we lost Tommy Johnson, Jeffrey Thomson, and Frank Steele. I remember that horrible night. I cursed God. There was no way a good and loving God would allow this evil to happen to this town, to this school, to this team, right before the championship game. When we started this game tonight, I tried to do things my way, and we fell apart. Then I finally gave in to Scrawny J's persistent requests to give him a chance. When he stepped out onto that field and he ran 74 yards for the touchdown, bypassing that defense that was kicking our ass every step of the way, I fell on my knees in tears. God has been knocking on the door of my heart, just asking that I give Him a chance to let go of my ways and my own understanding, and to trust that He knows what is best for me and that He loves me, and His ways are better than my own. Seeing Jimmy score that touchdown crushed me in every way, so that I could be rebuilt. Jimmy, I want to ask for your forgiveness personally. I know I don't deserve this, but could you please forgive me? And team, I hope you are seeing the lesson in what just happened with this game tonight. We need to believe in something greater than ourselves. When we trust in our own blind ambition, we fall apart. When we trust in something, or should I say Someone greater than ourselves, that is when we reach our full potential and receive blessings. I want to give the championship game ball to our brother, our MVP, Jimmy Jones!" Jimmy gave Coach Joe the biggest hug he had ever given. The whole team joined in one giant group hug, all cheering on Jimmy Jones! Jimmy knew that he would no longer be seen as Scrawny J and that he was finally seen. And inside Jimmy's heart, even though he had never given much thought to God, he now knew that God sees him, loves him, and has a plan and a purpose for his life.

CHAPTER 6

Jonathan Steele and Lisa Smith

After the championship game, of course, Jonathan was stoked that they had won the biggest game of the year, but there was a heaviness in his heart. He knew that his father would have been disappointed in his performance. The interceptions that Jonathan threw and all of the missed passes that he had thrown. He very well could have been the reason the Texas Rangers lost. Jonathan always needed his father's approval. Even though his father, Frank Steele, was a notorious drunk, he was still highly respected as the owner of Steele Manufacturing, which employed a majority of the community and was the leading manufacturer of steel used to make military weapons in all of Texas. His dad ran a tight ship, and it was beyond successful. Jonathan knew that he had to try to fill his father's shoes as he was to run the company once he got his master's degree in business. He could only imagine the chaos that was in the company right now. Also, he had carried the weight of what his mother was going through. She just lost her husband and almost lost her son due to drunken accidents. Jonathan's mom was a very timid woman, but she loved her son. He wanted to ensure that he was a good support for his mom and that Steele Manufacturing continued to thrive, thereby guaranteeing the family's success. He knew, even after the passing of his father, that he would punish himself with running drills and up-downs when he got home, but for now, he wanted to be mentally and spiritually present for the love of his life, Lisa Smith. After the game, Lisa went up to him to give him a big hug and congratulate him.

Lisa had been worried about Jonathan ever since the night of his car accident. Not only was she concerned about his physical well-being, but also his mental well-being. Lisa knew that Jonathan had not only lost two of his best friends but also his father. Even though his relationship with his dad was very complicated, and in her mind, toxic, she knew how much he loved and looked up to his dad. Lisa did not like sports one bit, but she went to all of Jonathan's games. She knew that he hadn't played his best and that he would be very hard on himself, but the emotions of this game were out of this world, and Jimmy's miracle performance left everyone in the stadium in awe. Lisa knew that Jimmy was the outcast of the team, and he was her kind of person. As a social justice warrior, she dedicated her life to fighting for the marginalized and the underrepresented. This was a significant moment in recognizing the worth of every single person, especially those who are often overlooked or ostracized. This was a huge win in her book, and she was extremely proud of Jonathan for how he treated Jimmy and appreciated his help in winning the game.

When Lisa came up to give Jonathan a huge congratulatory hug after the game, he felt led to say this, "Lisa, I know how broken I am and how much work I have to accomplish, but something felt different tonight. I don't know how much I believe in a god, but I could almost feel God's presence tonight. It made me realize that I can't live this life without you by my side. Would you take this journey with me forever, and would you be willing to be my future bride?" Lisa couldn't help but start crying and say, "Of course, you big idiot." With that being said, they had their very first kiss, it was as romantic and beautiful a kiss as a kiss could be. When everyone heard and saw this moment, they all stopped and cheered. This would forever be one of the best memories of their lives.

Jonathan had the biggest smile on his face. He still couldn't believe he just proposed to the love of his life. He had to stop for a moment to make sure he wasn't dreaming. He could foresee the rest of the school year, going to prom, and then this summer going on their camping trips. He had so much to look forward to. But when it was time to go home, he had walked back into his life's reality. Jonathan's mom was at home, lying face down on his parents' bed. He noticed an empty bottle of whiskey on the bedside table. He went up to her to see if she was alright, and she wasn't breathing. She didn't have a pulse. Jonathan realized that she had drunk herself to death. He dropped to his knees in complete and utter pain. He was so excited to share the news of his engagement with his mom, and now he finds her dead on her bed. He knew he had to call 911, and as the ambulance came and took her away, all he could feel was numb. Is happiness even possible for him? After an hour of just numbness, Jonathan went to his backyard in tears and started getting into position for sprints. He ran sprints until the sun rose that next morning and passed out in the grass. He woke up to Lisa running to him, asking what was going on, and she embraced him, and they cried together.

The following Friday, Lisa came to pick him up for his mother's funeral. Lisa was wearing a dress and came to help him tie his tie for his suit. Jonathan couldn't help but stay quiet that whole day. He did not know what to say or how even to feel. All that he knew was that he was grateful to have Lisa by his side. After the church service and finding himself at the grave site of his mom, next to his dad's already marked grave, it took all the strength that he could muster not to cry; his only comfort was having his hand held by her's. When they finally started to lower her body into the ground, all he could think to himself was, "I will make you guys proud, somehow."

After some time had passed and Jonathan was able to return to his regular school routine, things slowly started to hurt less, and he could be himself again. He was grateful for all the support he received from his friends, classmates, and the school. But most importantly, what kept him grounded was Lisa. They were both excited to talk about the upcoming Senior Prom. Provided by Steele Manufacturing, Jonathan was going to be able to get a limousine to pick up Lisa, go to a fantastic restaurant, and then walk side by side on the promenade together.

When the day of prom finally arrived, Lisa was over the moon excited. Jonathan has experienced many ups and downs. There were many times when he couldn't express any emotions, and it was painful to watch. Knowing everything that had happened lately, Jonathan had gone through hell and back, and Lisa was determined to be his support. But today, she is excited to leave behind all the pain and stress and just have fun with her fiancé on this prom day. Her dress was beautiful, and her mom was helping with her hair and makeup, and everything was going perfectly. She was going to be picked up in a limousine by "The" Jonathan Steele. She felt so blessed and so loved, and she was going to make sure that Jonathan felt this love today.

When they arrived at the restaurant, they couldn't help but laugh at how incredible the limo experience had already been. They sat on top of the fine leather seats that were more comfortable than anything they had felt before. They had top-of-the-line service with anything they could want to drink and some amazing hors d'oeuvres. They helped themselves to a bottle of champagne, and Jonathan poured their glasses. Jonathan and Lisa couldn't help but smile and laugh because they felt pretty badass being able to drink champagne even though they were underage. Lisa joked, saying, "There are privileges of being with a Steele, huh?" And Jonathan replied, "You can bet your bottom dollar there is." And they busted out laughing. Then they clanked their glasses together and cheered to the best prom night ever."

When they were seated at the restaurant, Lisa ordered her favorite dish of all time, Creamy Chicken Alfredo with breadsticks, and Jonathan ordered a New York Strip Steak cooked medium rare. After they placed their order, Lisa stared into Jonathan's eyes, one of those glances where Jonathan feels like she is staring into his very soul, and she said to him, "I love you with all of my heart, Jonathan Steele. I can't imagine doing this life without you. I want to be the best wife and mother, and I want to show you the kind of love that you've never received in your entire life. Through your hardships and through your failures, I want to prove to you that I will always be there. I know that it feels like everyone has left your side, leaving you broken. I want to be the person that you can put your trust and hope in. I love you so much, Jonathan Steele." Hearing Lisa say this made Jonathan tear up, and all he could do in that moment was smile and say, "I love you with all my heart, Lisa Smith. Forever and always." And then after a couple of minutes of them holding hands and looking at each other, Jonathan said, "Now, can we be done with all this ewy gooey stuff and have a fun night together?" Lisa chuckled and responded, "Hell yeah!"

After their delicious dinner, they got back into their fantastic limousine and treated themselves to another glass of champagne to loosen up for the big night ahead.

When they arrived at the school, they walked in hand in hand, and everyone greeted them. And they all had to get in line for the big prom walk. Jonathan and Lisa were told to get to the front of the line. When they started their walk, everyone in the gymnasium stood up from their seats and cheered for them. Jonathan and Lisa both got tears in their eyes, and Lisa realized she had to straighten up because she didn't want to ruin her makeup for pictures.

After everyone had made it through the prom line, all the parents came to give their hugs and offer good wishes for the night, and the party music began. And Lisa, even though these party scenarios were usually out of her element, let herself get loose and started dancing with Jonathan. They truly were having the night of their lives. All the brokenness lifted, and they were just happy being together. They were jumping up and down and just letting themselves be silly.

Then, after about an hour of dancing, it was time for the ceremony of crowning the Prom King and Queen. Principal Clark came up to the podium and started giving his speech.

"I want to thank everyone for being here at this wonderful celebration of Senior Prom this year. I hope and expect everyone to have a fun and responsible night. This has been a tough and challenging year for the school and the community. We lost two very inspirational and amazing students in our school, Tommy Johnson and Jeffrey Thomson. We also lost a very important person in our community, who happened to be the father of one of our students here tonight, Frank Steele, the father of our valued student, Jonathan Steele. There has been a lot of heartache and a lot of emotions going on in our community, and I want to make sure that we honor the lives that were lost way too soon. We have suffered loss in our community, but we have been able to come together as a community and have grown stronger together. We had a huge bonding moment as our varsity football team, the

Texas Rangers, won the championship game this year! It may just be a football game to some, but for our community, it showcased our strength, resilience, and ability to come together, unite, and grow. With that being said, I believe it is time to crown our Prom King and Queen! Who's ready to celebrate this moment?"

Everyone in the crowd erupted in cheer. Jonathan and Lisa were listening to Principal Clark's speech intensely while holding each other's hands. Lisa was hoping and praying that Jonathan would be crowned Prom King, while Jonathan was hoping and praying that Lisa would be crowned Prom Queen. The anticipation was out of control.

Principal Clark continued, "I love the energy! So without further ado, I would like to first present the Prom Queen crown to a very special young lady who, throughout her years in high school, has always been the one who will make sure everyone is having a good day, a powerful advocate for social justice who is leading the fight to end racism, sexism, injustice, and bullying in any way. During this challenging year in our school and community, we are all grateful and want to celebrate a woman like her who spreads love and positivity in bleak and seemingly hopeless times. This young lady is truly a beacon of light in the darkness. With all that being said, I would like to present to you all Ms. Lisa Smith as this year's Prom Queen! Let's give it up for her!"

Jonathan, in a very excited manner, jumped up and down when he heard that Lisa was being presented as this year's Prom Queen. Heaven knows she deserves this reward and every moment of recognition that she can get. He turned to Lisa, who was tearing up in shock and awe, and he gave her the biggest hug he could give, and they did a quick kiss before he said, "Well, what are you waiting for? Get your butt up there, Ms. Prom Queen!" Lisa gave him a playful jab to his shoulders and then said, "See your butt up there in a minute, Mr. Prom King." Jonathan responded, "You don't know that, haha!" She replied, "Wait and see." Of course, Lisa didn't know it for a fact, but deep in her soul, she knew that he would get the crown. Lisa was going to treasure every moment of this night. Things were finally going her way in this really challenging life, and she couldn't feel more blessed, and she knew she had Jonathan Steele to thank for all of this. He gave her the confidence to be herself and stand up for her beliefs. Lisa was head over heels in love with this man.

When Lisa reached the stage, Principal Clark shook her hand and gave her genuine congratulations, saying, "Thank you for all you do, you definitely deserve this!" He then crowned her as Prom Queen, and everyone in the crowd went crazy! Lisa couldn't help but give Principal Clark a big hug and said, "Thank you, Principal Clark, you are the best principal a community could ask for!"

After all of the celebration for Lisa, now it was time to hear who would get the coveted reward of this year's Prom King. As Principal Clark grabbed the microphone to start the announcement, the anticipation grew, and Lisa hoped and prayed that the pick would be Jonathan, because having her stand with anyone else would just feel wrong and incomplete. It would definitely take away from the perfect night having to dance with someone else for the "royal dance."

With the anticipation at full strength, Principal Clark started speaking, "As I've shared, this community has unfortunately struggled through so much heartbreak and terrible loss. But through terrible loss, we have grown stronger together. There is one young individual who arguably suffered the most severely in our community, yet has been a symbol of our resilience and strength. This young man was best friends with the two high school students whose names we'll never forget—Tommy

Johnson and Jeffrey Thomson, but this individual also suffered the loss of his father on that dreadful night. On top of that, the night of the big championship game came home to the passing of his mother. Not only was this family so important to our small-town community, but also to our school's sports organization. I cannot fathom the amount of pain this young man has endured in such a short period, but I also appreciate the strength and re-silience he has demonstrated to our school and community. Our hearts are with this young man. I would like to introduce to you all this year's Prom King—Jonathan Steele!"

The whole crowd cheered like crazy! As Jonathan was walking up to the stage, the other surviving member of the Quadruple Threat and Jonathan's last remaining best friend, Bobby Holt, came up to him to congratulate him and gave him a huge bro hug. On his way to the stage, everyone was trying to give him high fives and chant his name. Jonathan had no words. He loved this town and this community and was grateful for the support he had been given, but deep inside, Jonathan felt far from worthy. He always has his father's screams and critiques in his head. Even at the best of moments, Jonathan felt like he could never make his father proud, and he was haunted by this feeling every mo-ment of every day. The only thing that helped him the most in bringing him out of his own personal hell was waiting for him on that stage: the love of his life, Lisa Smith. Her smile just breaks him in the best way possible.

When he got on stage, Principal Clark gave Jonathan a long, firm handshake as he presented him the Prom King crown, and he said something in private to Jonathan that will stick with Jonathan till his last dying breath, "This world will do its best to leave you defeated. The adversary comes to steal, kill, and destroy, but the God of the Universe comes to give eternal life. No matter if you are standing strong or falling to your knees, the Father of the

Universe, who created every living thing, created you with a purpose. God doesn't expect perfection; all He asks for is a genuine relationship with you. Not some made-up version that makes you look good enough for His love or His grace, but the real, broken, and imperfect you. When we admit that we are lost and we allow God to be the light in our darkness, we will walk in forgiveness, love, hope, and purpose. Instead of judgment, we receive grace and mercy. When you feel unqualified due to your shortcomings or mistakes, I want you always to remember that God doesn't call the qualified but qualifies the called. Thank you, Jonathan, for all that you do for our community and our school. I hope and pray that God will use your life in unimaginable ways. I know right now you may not be able to see past the pain, but I promise that God will turn this pain into purpose."

After Principal Clark gave his private personal message to Jonathan, he then put the crown on Jonathan's head and declared to the crowd, "I present to you this year's Prom King and Queen!" And the whole gymnasium erupted in applause, and Jonathan and Lisa couldn't help in the midst of the cheer to give each other the most magical kiss as Prom King and Queen.

The rest of the evening was a magical blur. Jonathan and Lisa were just lost in heavenly awe. They danced the night away and took advantage of every moment.

After prom night, the rest of the school year seemed to fly by. Jonathan knew that he had to obtain a master's degree in business so that he could be in a position to start running his father's company, Steele Manufacturing. Although money was not an issue, he knew he could secure a full football scholarship. Jonathan always wanted to play college football, but the way his life was going, he was more focused on earning his degree so that he could start working at Steele Manufacturing and begin his life with Lisa, including getting married, buying a house, and starting a family. Lisa wanted to earn a degree in psychology to understand better what made people tick. That thought honestly scared Jonathan; he loved Lisa with all his heart, but he knew how broken he was, and he hated the idea of her digging more into his pain. Jonathan pictured their future with Lisa being a stay-at-home wife and mother. He knew that they wouldn't need a second income. Jonathan knew that this could really disappoint Lisa, but he would rather she not attend college and start a family instead. Jonathan knew that his father would want him to be the man of the house and raise hardworking men who would continue the family legacy with Steele Manufacturing.

Graduation day had finally arrived. Jonathan and Lisa were beyond excited for this day to come, so they could finally move forward with their future. With them having a high school engagement, they wanted to get married before Jonathan went off to college. They wanted to spend the summer having fun times together, with their special tradition of camping out, and then get married before Jonathan went off to college. Jonathan was able to meet Lisa's mother at graduation. He knew that Lisa's mother was a little bitter when it came to the Steele family because of the many hours and the considerable effort she had put into Steele Manufacturing. However, she understood how much Lisa loved Jonathan, and she wanted to give him a chance. Jonathan thought that the meeting had gone pretty well, and Lisa was glad that he had finally had the opportunity to meet her mother, especially on this momentous occasion, which marked the beginning of their lives together.

After all of the chaos that came with graduation day, Jonathan and Lisa saw no reason to wait for their first camping trip date. They gathered a tent, sleeping bags, lawn chairs, a charcoal grill, and camping sticks before heading to the local grocery store to

complete their shopping list. At the local grocery store, they pur-
chased the ingredients to make some awesome grilled cheeseburgers, everything to make S'mores, some charcoal, and some
firewood. But before they could leave, Jonathan had to work his
"Steele" magic and get a case of beer and a pack of cigarettes from
his college buddy, who worked at the grocery store. Jonathan and
Lisa had agreed to only smoke together while they were camping. For some reason, smoking a cigarette while having a beer at
the campfire was just the perfect symbol of the icing on the cake.
Jonathan and Lisa had spent their whole lives trying to please
others, so having beer and cigarettes together while camping was
their chance to rebel against the expectations that everyone had
put on them. They always looked forward to this. They would
sit together at the campfire after having some delicious grilled
cheeseburgers and not forget the S'mores for dessert. After having full and satisfied bellies, they would get drunk on beer and
have a few cigarettes while gazing into the campfire and at each
other, reminiscing about memories, both good and bad, and discussing their hopes and dreams. This was like therapy for them,
but these moments also created memories that they will never
forget.

After visiting the grocery store, they arrived at their all-time
favorite camping spot, a secluded area surrounded by trees
and located right on the lake that overlooked the campground.
Jonathan set up the tent, while Lisa prepared the sleeping bags
and arranged the food for when the grill was ready. After the
campsite was set up, Jonathan lit the campfire and the grill, and
the night was getting started. They looked into each other's eyes
to treasure the moment, and then after a minute, they couldn't
help but laugh at each other in excitement. Jonathan grilled the
burgers, and they put them on the buns with their toppings, then
opened their first beer. They almost forgot how awesome these
grilled burgers were. They very rarely had such excellent grilled

food. Jonathan always had to watch what he ate for football, and Lisa always tried to eat healthily, so these burgers were a real treat for them. Then came the ooey-gooey S'mores with golden, crisped marshmallows. After the first bite, they were in heaven. Once they finished the S'mores, they opened another beer, and they both lit up a cigarette, coughing and laughing. Lisa said, "We are sure badass, aren't we, Mr. Steele?" Jonathan responded, "We are the definition of badass!" And they laughed out loud. Then they both cheered for graduating.

As the night got later and a few beers deep, they were both glaring into the campfire, and they started to dig into a deep conversation. Lisa expressed her feelings about her father and her twin brother leaving her mother and her behind. She hated that her mom had to support them by herself. She knew that football was important to Jonathan, but she expressed her distaste for sports due to her father and brother. Jonathan started thinking about the loss of his father and his mother, but he didn't have enough to drink to express the pain that he was carrying. Even with Lisa, he found it impossible to discuss his internal need to continue trying to make his father proud. He instead started talking about his dream of finishing college, buying a house, and starting a family. He expressed that he could not bring himself to want to raise a family in his parents' home. He planned to use some funds from Steele Manufacturing to buy them a house, and he thought that they could give his parents' house to her mom. He wanted to show his appreciation to Lisa for being there for him through everything by giving her mother the house. When Lisa heard that Jonathan would give her mother their house, tears welled up in her eyes. Jonathan knew that he had a lot going on internally, but no matter how much he was hurting, he full-heartedly loved Lisa, and he would do everything he could to let her know that. Jonathan shared that he thought they would buy a house before he went off to college, one that would be fitting for their future family. He envisioned her living there to prepare, and he would come back on weekends to be with her. Without him saying it, Lisa knew that this meant that she would not be able to pursue her degree in psychology, but she was so lovestruck that she was willing to give that up to be Jonathan's wife and the mother to his children.

After a few more beers, they were definitely feeling the effects. After a while of being mushy and emotional, they decided to spend the rest of the night having fun and enjoying each other's company while drunk. They started playing their favorite songs, dancing together, being silly, smoking cigarettes, and enjoying the night. This was truly the perfect night to remember.

CHAPTER 7

Jimmy Jones and Coach Joe

That night after the most exciting game of his whole life, Jimmy went home in total shock and awe. Part of him could not fathom what had just happened that night of the championship game. The stars finally aligned in his favor. After taking hit after hit in every aspect of his life, Jimmy finally felt recognized and seen. But more than that, Jimmy felt like his deepest prayer was finally answered. From his homelife struggles with his single mom trying to take care of them to the abuse that he had to endure at school, it felt like God finally answered his prayer. Before Jimmy started his favorite routine of having pizza, pop, and popcorn while watching *The Twilight Zone* to celebrate, Jimmy felt called to read his Bible.

Growing up before his dad passed away, Jimmy's parents would often read him the book of Psalms in the Old Testament of the Bible. So, he decided to open the book of Psalms, and chapters 56 and 57 stood out to him. These chapters are about trusting in God through persecution. There were these verses that really hit Jimmy to his core. In Psalm chapter 56, verses 8 through 13: "You have kept count of my tossings; put my tears in Your bottle. Are they not in Your record? Then my enemies will retreat in the day when I call. This I know, that God is for me. In God, whose word I praise, in the Lord, whose word I praise, in God I trust; I am not afraid. What can a mere mortal do to me? My vows to You I must perform, O God; I will render thank offerings to You. For You have delivered my soul from death, and my feet from falling, so that I may walk before God in the light of life." Jimmy felt God's presence through these verses. These verses in the book of Psalms showed Jimmy that God saw every hardship he endured and was with him through it all, catching his tears when they fell. Jimmy knew that God walked with him through all of it, and God answered his prayers that night, rescuing him from the trials of his enemies. Jimmy also knew that he wanted to dedicate his life to service and gratitude to God for everything He had done for him. After spending some time in prayer, Jimmy headed to the kitchen to start preparing for his favorite pastime: pizza, popcorn, and pop, so that he could enjoy his night watching *The Twilight Zone*. But as he got everything prepared and put on *The Twilight Zone,* Jimmy couldn't stop thinking about that championship game and how God had answered his prayers.

After that championship game, Coach Joe never felt so much uncertainty in his life. It was after that game years ago, when every bone was broken in his knee, that he acknowledged his future would not be in the NFL. But this time, it wasn't the sense of hopelessness he felt after that game years before; instead, it was a moral awakening—like there was something out there, some sense of meaning that was bigger than himself. Scrawny J, actually Jimmy Jones, after all that he had put him through, was the reason that his team won that championship game. No one could have ever predicted that. There had to be a higher plan, a higher purpose than anything he had ever known before.

Coach Joe was always familiar with church and God. He was raised in a small Texas town, for God's sake, where everyone got drunk on Saturday night and woke up first thing on Sunday morning to go to church. His parents had a traditional picture of Jesus hanging right in the middle of their living room where he grew up. That picture always creeped him out. A picture of Jesus kneeling with His hands together in prayer with an angelic halo around His head, looking to the sky. He always thought it was just an old-fashioned religious fairy tale used to ensure kids behaved. Every time he took the Lord's name in vain or misbehaved in church, he either got his ass whooped by his dad's belt or got sent to his room for the evening by his mother. But maybe there was something more to this than some old wives' tale; maybe there was some truth behind this religious fairy tale.

Whatever the truth was, Coach Joe had a really convicting feeling that he needed to make up for all the mistreatment he had caused Jimmy. He had the idea of inviting Jimmy to church. With the game being on a Friday night, he figured he could ask Jimmy's mother tomorrow about taking her son to church and out to lunch on Sunday as a thank you for being such a tremendous help this season. So that is what he did. Coach Joe got up a little hungover that Saturday morning and decided he should do his three morning S's—Shit, Shave, and Shower, and got to his car and headed to Jimmy Jones' house. He was a bit nervous about talking to Jimmy's mom, but when he got to their door, Jimmy came out and was excited to see him. That gave Coach Joe a better start in terms of confidence. Jimmy's mom came to the door, sending Jimmy to his room, and then Coach Joe took a deep breath and said to his mom, "Hello, Mrs. Jones, I just wanted to come by this morning and thank you for allowing your son Jimmy to be a valuable part of this year's football team. I apologize that he didn't have as much field time as he would have liked, but he certainly was a crucial part of our victory in the championship game. I have seen a lot of football in my day, and Ma'am, your son played some of the best football I have ever seen in my life. So, Ma'am, I wanted to offer my sincere thanks and see if I can offer to take Jimmy to this Sunday morning's church service and out to lunch afterwards. Would that be alright with you?"

Jimmy's mother responded with, "I appreciate you taking the time to come out here and tell me that. I feel so bad about how much I have to work after the passing of my husband and his father that I can't see my little Jimmy play. Football is all he ever talks about. That would be very kind of you, Coach Joe. I'm sure that he would like that very much. What time should he be ready tomorrow morning?" Coach Joe responded, "No problem at all, Ma'am. With church at 10 a.m., I would be able to be here around 9:30," she replied. "That sounds like a plan, thank you again, Coach Joe. I will be sure to let Jimmy know." They both nodded, and Coach Joe got back to his car.

It was Sunday morning, and Coach Joe was coming to pick up Jimmy for church and lunch. Never in a thousand years could Jimmy have guessed that he would get to spend time with Coach Joe, and now Coach Joe had actually gone to his house, asking his mom for permission to take him to church and to lunch. Miracles happen every day! Jimmy put on one of his nice, churchlike shirts and a pair of nice pants. He was wondering if he should bring his Bible, and he decided, why not. He always enjoyed reading his own Bible, and if he wanted to make a note, he could do so. As he was finishing getting his church clothes on, he heard the doorbell, and it was Coach Joe. He grabbed his Bible and ran to the front door in the living room. He quickly slipped on his shoes and answered the door. Coach Joe said, "Good morning, buddy, are you ready to go?" Jimmy responded with an excited "Yes, sir." Coach Joe said, "You can call me Joe." Jimmy was both nervous and excited, as they got into the car.

After he backed out of the driveway and put the car into drive, Coach Joe said, "I wanted to thank you for coming to church with me today. I haven't been in years, and I didn't really want to go alone. I don't really know how to say this, but after that championship game and seeing you play ball, my whole reality flipped upside down. With all this injustice in this dog-eat-dog world, I always believed I needed to rely on myself and no one else, and I had to be the best and strongest person that I could be. Emotions were a weakness. Church and God always seemed like some fairy tale that my parents used to get us to behave. But that moment you made that 74-yard touchdown, everything that I believed was shattered to pieces. I believe that God has a plan for you, and I want to get to know the God that allowed that moment to happen." Jimmy responded, "I always dreamed of playing football, and I always gave it my best, but I guess I never knew that big moment of my dreams would actually happen. I was blinded by the lies that I was no good and I would never be enough. After my father passed away and my mother became the sole breadwinner, I always thought we would struggle just to get by, and there was nothing that I could do because I'm just Scrawny J. But God answered my prayers that night, and I am excited to get to go to church with my hero, Coach Joe." Coach Joe couldn't really say much after that; he tried to hide that he was tearing up a bit, but he responded, "Well, thank you, I'm excited too."

When they pulled up to the church, they were both a bit nervous. Neither Coach Joe nor Jimmy had been to church in years, and they did not know what to expect. When they arrived at the entry doors, they were greeted by a greeter who welcomed them to the church and handed them both a church bulletin. There was a coffee table area in the lobby right when you walked in, but there were a bunch of people visiting over there, so Jimmy and Coach Joe decided to sneak into the sanctuary, and they got a seat toward the back. They both remembered the church pews. In the pews, they had a Bible and a hymnal book where they were seated. Coach Joe, out of awkwardness of being in the church, grabbed the Hymnal book and just kind of browsed the pages. Then the worship choir started, and a girl who was singing in the choir caught Jimmy's eye. They were singing beautiful songs about God. Then the girl that caught Jimmy's eye had a solo during the start of a hymn that Jimmy had never heard before. The song was called "Amazing Grace." Her beautiful voice astounded Jimmy, and then he heard the words.

"Amazing grace! How sweet the sound
That saved a wretch like me!
I once was lost, but now I'm found;
Was blind, but now I see.
'Twas grace that taught my heart to fear,
And grace my fears relieved;
How precious did that grace appear
The hour I first believed."

Jimmy couldn't help but start crying when he heard the lyrics of that song. For so long, he never felt like he was enough. His father passed away, and his mother gave up everything so that he could survive. Everyone on the football team and at school talked down to him, bullied him, and made him feel like he was nothing. He was lost, but now he sees and knows that God sees him, God loves him, and God has a plan and a purpose for his life. How precious that moment when he finally rushed past all the gigantic football players and got that 74-yard touchdown, how precious that moment when he first believed.

Coach Joe was definitely out of his element being at this church service. Coach Joe had always lived and breathed football. Always trying to become number one, the best of the best. But sitting to his left, Jimmy had changed everything in his life and everything that he had ever believed. The choir was playing a hymn that he had heard as a child, called "Amazing Grace," and the message of this song must have really resonated with Jimmy because he was crying. Coach Joe was still, just sitting and trying to process everything. He was uncomfortable, but he really wanted to give this a chance. After the song "Amazing Grace," the choir disbanded, and the pastor came up to the preacher's booth. The pastor thanked the choir and welcomed everyone to church.

When the preacher started to speak, Coach Joe really made sure to listen intently. The preacher started the sermon with this Bible verse—Philippians 2:5–8: "Let the same mind be in you that was in Christ Jesus, who, though He was in the form of God, did not regard equality with God as something to be exploited, but emptied Himself, taking the form of a slave, being born in human likeness. And being found in human form, He humbled Himself and became obedient to the point of death—even death on a cross." Coach Joe never heard anything like this. He never considered God as a representation of humility. Humility always felt like a weakness. You have to be strong; you have to be the best to be seen and heard. Everything about this is flipping Coach Joe's perspective upside down. And then the preacher shared this story from the Bible: Matthew 20:1–16—"For the kingdom of heaven is like a landowner who went out early in the morning to hire laborers for his vineyard. After agreeing with the laborers for the usual daily wage, he sent them into his vineyard. When he went out about nine o'clock, he saw others standing idle in the marketplace; and he said to them, 'You also go into the vineyard, and I will pay you whatever is right.' So they went. When he went out again about noon and about three o'clock, he did the same. And about five o'clock, he went out and found others standing around; and he said to them, 'Why are you standing here idle all day?' They said to him, 'Because no one has hired us.' He said to them, 'You also go into the vineyard.' When evening came, the owner of the vineyard said to his manager, 'Call the laborers and give them their pay, beginning with the last and then going to the first.' When those hired about five o'clock came, each of them received the usual daily wage. Now, when the first came, they thought they would receive more, but each of them also received the usual daily wage. And when they received it, they grumbled against the landowner, saying, 'These last worked only one hour, and you have made them equal to us who have borne the burden of the day and the scorching heat.' But he replied to one of them, 'Friend, I am doing you no wrong; did you not agree with me for the usual daily wage? Take what belongs to you and go; I choose to give to this last the same as I give to you. Am I not allowed to do what I choose with what belongs to me? Or are you envious because I am generous?' So the last will be first, and the first will be last." This story literally left Coach Joe's mouth open. Was the worker who worked one hour paid the same amount as the worker who worked all day?! There is no way this story could be true. He was utterly speechless. The final bit of Bible scripture the preacher used was from Ephesians 2:8–9: "For by grace you have been saved through faith, and this is not your own doing, it is the gift of God—not the result of works, so that no one may boast." This was Coach Joe's breaking point. He started to cry. Every damn day, he worked his ass off to be the best, to be good enough, but God loves him no matter what he does. In fact, God loves him despite what he has done. He never had unconditional love. His family judged him and made him earn his worth. He always had to earn people's love and respect. But through all of his failures, through all of his shortcomings, God still loves him. He doesn't have to earn it. God used Scrawny J to cut his ego and his pride completely, and it utterly broke him. But God didn't humble him to humiliate him, but to show him that God still loves him, no matter what. God loves unconditionally. Coach Joe's internal barriers just shattered in that moment, and tears rushed down his cheeks.

As Jimmy sat next to Coach Joe and listened to the preacher's sermon, he couldn't help but feel God's presence in this moment. The preacher spoke with such conviction and truth. He was sharing about God's love and grace in our lives, as well as the importance of humility. He then went on to share these verses, which really resonated with Jimmy. John 15:1–7,12–14: "I am the true vine, and My Father is the vinegrower. He removes every branch in Me that bears no fruit. Every branch that bears fruit, he prunes to make it bear more fruit. You have already been cleansed by the word that I have spoken to you. Abide in Me and I abide in you. Just as the branch cannot bear fruit by itself unless it abides in the vine, neither can you unless you abide in Me. I am the vine, you are the branches. Those who abide in Me and I in them bear much fruit because apart from Me you can do nothing. Whoever does not abide in Me is thrown away like a branch and withers; such branches are gathered, thrown into the fire, and burned. If you abide in Me, and My words abide in you, ask for whatever you wish, and it will be done for you. (12) This is My commandment, that you love one another as I have loved you. No one has greater love than this, to lay down one's life for one's friends. You are my friends if you do what I command you." These verses really impacted Jimmy. He never really knew true love, but he always strived for love and to be enough. To be recognized and to be seen. God desires us to bear fruit, but we cannot bear fruit apart from the vine. When we abide by God's commandments, not only are we saved, but we become fruitful and we are friends of God. Friends who He is willing to die for. How beautiful and how humbling. It felt like God was directly speaking to the deepest parts of his soul. He desired with every part of his being to be a fruit-bearing friend of God. He wanted to make a difference and love others the way that God has loved him.

After this convicting and soul-wrenching church service, Coach Joe and Jimmy went to the local diner for lunch. They both really didn't know what to say after that spiritual and emotional roller coaster they just went through, so to lighten the mood, Coach Joe said to Jimmy, "That choir girl sure seemed to catch your eye, huh, kid? Haha," Jimmy smirked and said, "Yeah, she was pretty cute, and she seemed actually to see me, haha." Coach Joe responded, "What's not to see!" They both laughed, although Jimmy got a red face from embarrassment.

Once they had their food, Coach Joe suggested that they discuss what they had taken away from the church service. Since it was his suggestion, Coach Joe started the conversation, "As you know, I have always lived and breathed football. I was a perfectionist. I not only had to be good enough, but I also had to be the best. Anything but the best was weakness. Today I learned that we don't have to earn God's love. Even while we were sinners, God sent His Son to die for us so that we can be saved. If we acknowledge that we are lost and that we have messed up and ask for forgiveness, we can be set free and become children of God. Damn, did I need that, Jimmy! And I'll be damned if I don't make it my life's purpose to share that love and that truth with everyone that I meet. This changed me, Jimmy, and I have to thank you for being a major part of this heart change for me." Jimmy responded, "In a lot of ways, we are similar, Coach Joe. After my dad died, I always wanted to be enough for everyone. I wanted to be enough for my mom, I wanted to make my dad proud, I wanted to be enough for the football team, and for you. I wanted to be seen as an incredible running back. I wanted to be seen, to have a plan and a purpose for my life, but all I received was pain and brokenness. Today, I learned that I do have a plan and purpose for my life, but not by becoming enough, because on my own, I can never be enough. However, through Jesus and His love and grace, by sacrificing Himself for my salvation, I am God's child. As the words of the hymn "Amazing Grace": *"Amazing Grace! How sweet the sound that saved a wretch like me!"* But the words that God really placed on my heart were these words from that hymn: *"I once was lost, but now I'm found; was blind, but now I see."*

PART 2

20 Years Later

CHAPTER 8

Mr. and Mrs. Steele

Mrs. Steele

The good ol' high school days seemed like a lifetime ago for Lisa Steele, as she has become a mother to three children and the wife of the most successful businessman in town, Jonathan Steele. They had a lovely home with beautiful children; the oldest was Tommy Frank Steele, the second son was Jeffrey Joe Steele, and the third child was their only daughter, Jessica-Ann Steele. Tommy and Jeffrey were named after the two members of the Quadruple Threat who passed away the year of the big championship game. Even though Jonathan had been too busy to keep in touch with the other surviving member of the Quadruple Threat, Bobby Holt, he always loved reliving the glory days. He wanted to keep the memory of the unstoppable Quadruple Threat alive. Their son Tommy's middle name, Frank, is in memory of Jonathan's father, and Jeffrey's middle name, Joe, is in respect to one of Jonathan's most incredible role models in the world, Coach Joe. Their daughter, Jessica-Ann, was named by both Jonathan and Lisa; Lisa simply loved the name Jessica, and Ann was in memory of Jonathan's mother.

The year of that big championship game is always stuck in Jonathan's mind. That year definitely impacted him, with the loss of his parents, as well as the big win of the championship game. He lived his whole life from that night on, trying to make his parents proud. Often, Lisa wished that Jonathan would learn to live in the present. His ego grew significantly in high school, but Lisa knew that there were also deep wounds from that year. Lisa was very grateful that they had a beautiful house, three beautiful children, and that Jonathan kept his word and let her mom move into his parents' home. Lisa was happy that her mom's needs were taken care of, but Lisa often felt alone in this marriage. If Jonathan wasn't trying to teach their sons football, he was at work or at "business meetings" with "his boys," which meant his work friends. Lisa wasn't stupid; she knew that the "business meetings" were nights out at the bar with his work friends, and that left her alone with all of the chores and feeling like she was raising these kids by herself. Many nights, Lisa dreamed about her long-held dream of attending college for psychology and being able to make a difference as a counselor. Still, then she thought to herself, how could she help anyone else when her own husband had so many internal scars that he would never open up about? One of the only things that kept Lisa sane was being able to call her mother at night to vent about her frustrations. Those phone calls with her mother were about the only thing that kept her going. Lisa's mother, after she was able to move into her new home and retire, began reading the Bible and was radically saved by the grace of God. Lisa didn't know what she believed about God, but she loved seeing the transformation in her mother and had a desire to discuss it with her. Her mom would often read Bible verses to her over the phone, which really helped her in times of trial and desperation. Lisa frequently believed that if God were real and would soften her husband's heart, there would be no greater miracle for her to witness, and that would be all the proof she would need to believe. Even though Jonathan never hit Lisa, he would verbally abuse her, especially on the nights that he came home drunk. Lisa often thought about the beautiful nights she used to spend with Jonathan around the campfire, sharing beers and cigarettes, just to enjoy each other's company, have genuine conversations, and have fun together. She missed those days, but now his whole life was being the best CEO of Steele Manufacturing, making sure his sons were the best football players they could be, and being drunk with "the boys." It felt like she was just a burden in his way nowadays.

Lisa always had an internal connection with Jonathan, and she knew when he wasn't doing alright. However, as the years went on and his internal wounds deepened, she realized that her words did less and less to help Jonathan. Sometimes she wondered if her talent and passion for helping the hurting, broken, and marginalized were being drained and wasted on her husband. She often daydreamed about what her life would have looked like if she had attended college after high school and pursued her dreams instead of trying to heal Jonathan. She hated the distance that came between them after he went away to college and started seriously pursuing his goal of becoming the CEO of Steele Manufacturing. Lisa had always hated Steele Manufacturing since she was a young girl, watching her mom waste away while trying to be a single mother and slaving away for a company that didn't care for her. For the higher-ups, which unfortunately included her husband, it was all about the power and the wealth, never about the ordinary workers who made the manufacturing actually possible. Lisa felt like her way of life is funded by the enemy, greedy, hungry elites. This knowledge really ate at Lisa's soul, but more than that, she knew that her husband had not only fallen victim to this mindset, but his soul had been sucked into this evil corporation. Lisa often would reflect on Bible verses that her mom shared with her:

1 Timothy 6:6–10:

> Of course, there is great gain in godliness com-
> bined with contentment; for we brought nothing
> into the world, so that we can take nothing out
> of it; but if we have food and clothing, we will be
> content with these. But those who want to be rich
> fall into temptation and are trapped by senseless
> and harmful desires that plunge people into ruin
> and destruction. For the love of money is a root
> of all kinds of evil, and in their eagerness to be
> rich, some have wandered away from the faith
> and pierced themselves with many pains.

Luke 14:11:

> For all who exalt themselves will be humbled, and
> those who humble themselves will be exalted.

Matthew 11:28–30:

> Come to Me, all you that are weary and are carry-
> ing heavy burdens, and I will give you rest. Take
> My yoke upon you, and learn from Me; for I am
> gentle and humble in heart, and you will find rest
> for your souls. For My yoke is easy, and My bur-
> den is light.

Lisa knew that Jonathan was a victim of power and greed, but she
also knew that in his heart, Jonathan was carrying a multitude of
heavy burdens. He is drowning in the weight of trying to be good
enough. Lisa couldn't help but think that maybe we are all just
lost children that need to be found by the Heavenly Father.

Mr. Steele

Jonathan has been so sick and tired of his wife's nagging. Everything that he does is to make their family better. He works his ass off at work to bring in a major check to ensure that his family has everything they need and to ensure that their children will be able to go to great colleges and have a great future. Yes, he is hard on their sons, but to become the best football players, they have to work their asses off. He remembered all the training and workouts he had done to become the best. Hard work never hurts anyone. Jonathan hated the nagging about him going to business meetings with the boys at the bar. How else was he supposed to let off the pressure of every day of his life? Having a drink with the boys was the only time he felt like he could have fun.

Additionally, they discussed business, making it consistently productive. Jonathan hated it when he got home, and Lisa would talk about her mom and the Bible. Like God ever did anything for him. He took his parents away when he was in high school, leaving him on his own. What good God is that? Jonathan had to walk past this homeless beggar who loved to sit at the corner of the street by his office door. It really got to him the irony of this blind homeless beggar's sign: "I once was blind, but now I see. Would you please help me?" It was almost ironic that this blind man's sign says he once was blind, but now he sees. Well, it would be entertaining if it weren't so irritating that this homeless guy always greeted him and told him that God loves him. *Yeah, God must really love you, huh, buddy? Being blind and homeless on the street is a sure sign that there's a loving God, huh?* Another thing that really got under Jonathan's skin was that he could almost see his old high school football teammate in this homeless guy. Beneath the sunglasses, the old, baggy, torn-up clothes, and the wrinkles of his skin, it almost felt like it could be ol' Scrawny J. Well, actually, after the amazing championship game of his senior year of high school, Jonathan promised himself he would never refer to him as Scrawny J again, but Jimmy Jones. But there was no way that this blind homeless guy could be the same guy who ran that 74-yard touchdown in his senior year championship game. No way in hell that could be Jimmy Jones.

Jonathan never stopped loving his wife, Lisa, but damn the amount of disrespect that she gives him. What more could he do for her? He gave his parents' house to Lisa's mom, who is always on call with Lisa talking about this "good God" guy, and he still felt like they always badmouthed him and Steele Manufacturing, which is the sole reason that they have as good a life as they have. But heaven forbid, he works there and will have drinks with the boys.

To be honest, the drinking wasn't always about having fun for Jonathan. It often numbed the pain that he didn't want to be constantly running through his mind. He never could let go of the image of the moment he found out his dad died, and the moment he walked home to see his mom had overdosed and passed away at their home. He always wanted to make his parents proud. He lived his whole life trying to be good enough for his father, but he will never get to hear those words, *"I'm proud of you,"* from his father, and that fact has pretty much driven him to be numb. He appreciated Lisa and how much she has done for him, but nothing and no one can ever make up for the fact that his father died, and he never made his father proud.

CHAPTER 9

Jimmy Jones

A lot has happened for Jimmy Jones since that day at church twenty years ago with Coach Joe. Jimmy had a rich life and experienced many ups and downs in his faith journey, but through it all, he knew that God was always watching over him and never left him. Jimmy truly believed that God had a plan and a purpose for his life; however, it was way more challenging than he could have ever predicted. Jimmy did end up marrying that beautiful choir girl, whose name was Ashley, from the church that he attended with Coach Joe that day. Jimmy and Ashley got married, and then Jimmy enrolled in the military. She ended up becoming pregnant, and she was to deliver their first child before he enlisted in the military. Ashley unfortunately died in childbirth, but she delivered a beautiful baby girl who was named Grace. Jimmy was devastated that Ashley passed away, and he knew that he could not take care of Grace, especially since he was supposed to go overseas with the military. So, Jimmy made the difficult decision to give custody of Grace to Ashley's parents. Then he was deployed to the Middle East to fight in the Iraq War; there, he lost his vision in a bomb explosion and was medically discharged from the military. He was shipped back to his hometown, where he was homeless. Jimmy became really depressed and didn't want to show his face to anyone. He turned to drinking and quickly became addicted to numb the pain. Jimmy felt like he had lost everything. He lost his wife, he gave up his daughter, and he saw so much bloodshed and death in war. Jimmy had reached his lowest point in life at this point. He pretty much planned on drinking himself to death. He became homeless, and every dime that he received turned into money to put into a whiskey bottle.

One night, Jimmy got so drunk and so depressed that he decided that he would end it all. That night, he brought his bottle of booze to the town's traffic bridge, feeling the ledge with his hands, he lifted himself on the edge, and was going to jump. In his tears, he decided to cry out to God, saying, "I thought you had a plan for me. I thought you loved me. Now I'm blind, I'm alone, and have nothing to live for. God, give me one reason not to end my life right here and now; otherwise, I am going to jump and end it all." In that moment, he heard the voice of an angel singing the song he had heard that first day at church from his future wife. The angelic voice behind him sang these words:

> Amazing grace! How sweet the sound
> That saved a wretch like me!
> I once was lost, but now I'm found;
> Was blind, but now I see.
> 'Twas grace that taught my heart to fear,
> And grace, my fears relieved;
> How precious did that grace appear
> The hour I first believed

Jimmy could not believe his senses. He turned back, and that same voice called to him and said, "Dad, I am here. I'm your daughter, Grace. Don't jump, don't jump!" She ran up to him and embraced him, and they both bursted into tears. In shock and awe, Jimmy asked, "Grace?! How are you here? How did you know I was here? What is this? Are you real? Are you really here?" In great relief, Grace responded, "I have been going to a church led by Pastor Joe named 'Pursuing Freedom Non-Denominational Church,' with my family. Through Jesus Christ, I have received the gift of forgiveness and salvation, and tonight I felt spiritually led to search for you." For many years, I resented God and you for abandoning me after my mom died giving birth to me. I have struggled with insecurities and trying to be strong on my own, striving for perfection, but I could never overcome them. Still, then I heard this story at church from Pastor Joe portraying God as a shepherd of a hundred sheep. The Shepherd cared for each individual sheep that when one sheep got lost, he left the ninety-nine sheep to rescue and restore the one lost sheep; and, at that point, I accepted Jesus as my Savior. I have been forgiven, and I have decided to forgive you; I want to restore our relationship. We all have a past, and we all need God's forgiveness.

"Most importantly, God loves each and every one of His children and wants to bring us home. Dad, I have come to rescue you and bring you home to be among God's children." Through Jimmy's tears, he said to Grace, "Do you know how I met your mother and why we named you Grace? I went to church with my high school football coach, Coach Joe, and that was the day I gave my life to Jesus. It was also the day I first saw your mother. She was in the choir and was singing the hymn you were just singing, 'Amazing Grace.' I'm sorry, Grace, for leaving you. I didn't know what to do, and I was hurting when I lost your mother, and I wasn't ready to be a single father, and I did what I believed was best for you. I have fallen from grace in so many ways. I don't know what to say but thank you from the bottom of my heart."

Jimmy and Grace, in tears, both embraced each other and held on for dear life. Grace then helped her dad up and took him to the nearest coffee shop to warm him up and so that they could talk more. Grace told her dad about her life living with her grandparents and how she was a basketball player and a member of the choir, just like her mom. She told him about her dream to attend college for Youth Ministry, aiming to help young people in their relationship with God. Jimmy was overjoyed and almost in disbelief that he was, in this moment, having coffee with his daughter, and marveling at how much she had accomplished in her life. He was not ready to tell her that he was homeless. He couldn't bear to put that burden on her, but he truly received the answer to his prayers, and he felt God's loving embrace in that very moment. Jimmy knew he wanted to start living for his Savior again. He strayed from the path for so long, but God never left him. He was taken back to the moment he scored that 74-yard touchdown, and for the first time in his life, he felt recognized and seen, as if God had actually heard his prayers. At this moment, he is experiencing the same overwhelming love from God that he felt twenty years ago when he made that life-altering touchdown in the championship game.

After they finished their coffee and talked for quite a while, Jimmy promised Grace that he would come with her to church sometime. He knew that he was still not her legal guardian, and he did not want to overstep his bounds, but he walked away feeling like a new man, with newfound hope. When Grace went back home, Jimmy went to his usual alley to sleep, and as he lay down, he prayed to God to please use his life to bless others and to be the father that Grace deserves.

That next morning, Jimmy felt led to hold up the sign that he had previously made with the help of a fellow homeless man, that read: *"I once was blind but now I see. Would you please help me?"* With his sign, his hope and prayer was that God would allow the opportunity to share his story, and maybe the donations he could receive would help him get back on a better track to be the man and the father that Grace deserved.

As Jimmy sat in the alley with his sign, he began to notice someone who seemed very familiar. Of course, he couldn't see this guy, but his voice had something that sounded so familiar. He couldn't bring himself to believe it, but Jimmy could almost swear it sounded like his old quarterback from his football team, Jonathan Steele. Every morning, this guy would walk past him on his way to work, and every day at 5 p.m., he would walk past him again, often discussing plans to go out drinking with his co-workers. But every time he walked past Jimmy, he felt this glare of discomfort. Jimmy didn't know if it was because of his ironic sign that read *"I once was blind but now I see. Would you please help me?"* Jimmy knew the sign was ironic because, of course, he is blind, but with God's love, mercy, and grace, he can now truly see. So, Jimmy didn't know if the guy was glaring at him because of his sign or because he was homeless on the street, but Jimmy felt called to pray for him every time he walked past. Hopefully, with his prayers and the conviction of the Holy Spirit, perhaps that was the real reason for the uncomfortable glares. Jimmy knew that God uses every situation for His own good and for those who are called according to His purpose. If Jimmy could be used as part of God's plan, that would be incredible. Jimmy always wanted to be part of something greater than himself, and he has now realized that as he walks in faith with Jesus on his spiritual journey, it is then that true meaning and purpose truly emerge. He definitely did not end up where he thought he would be as he sits blind and homeless in a city alley, but he knows that God sees him, and as it says in Romans 8:28, "We know that all things work together for good for those who love God, who are called according to His purpose." With that promise, no matter what happens, whether he lives and breathes or passes away,

Jimmy knows that he lives to honor and serve God, and that is how one truly lives a life that is bigger than one's self.

CHAPTER 10

Pastor Joe

Waking up on this Sunday morning, Joe couldn't help but think about how the life he is living is different from the life he thought he would have lived. His life went from everyone calling him Coach Joe to now being known as "Pastor Joe." Every time he hears *"Pastor Joe,"* it just leaves him in awe.

He remembered the conversation he had with Principal Clark before the championship game, in which he was told that if he could win the big game, he would receive a 20 percent raise in his salary. Then that awful night happened, when they lost two core members of the Quadruple Threat, and he remembered in that moment losing all hope. But then, the unbelievable happened: Scrawny J scored a 74-yard touchdown and then won the game for us. That moment will forever live in his memory. But it was so much more than that championship game; it was a spiritual awakening for Joe. His whole life flipped upside down in that moment, and then that first church service he went to with Jimmy. From that moment on, he was freed from chasing approval and perfection. He no longer had to earn his worth or his value. He felt the love, mercy, and grace of God fill his soul and enter into every fiber of his being. He learned the value of humility and grace.

Despite his imperfections, he is worth dying for. He was truly re-born that day and gave his life to Jesus. He could no longer coach football after that experience. He needed to spread the love and truth of the Gospel. He gave up his salary raise and his passion for football to pursue ministry. Instead of teaching football to these kids, he wanted to bring families together and bring unity, love, and truth. He wanted to share God's love with anyone who struggled as he did.

One thing that Joe knew he wanted was to bring about change in the church he wanted to start, getting rid of all the religious stigma that he had been raised to believe. He tried to make room for everyone, regardless of their past. Instead of worship-ing some far-out figure in the sky that wants to strike you dead for any mistake you might make, he wanted to bring to light the one true God that wants a relationship with you, no matter your past mistakes or the baggage you might carry. Instead of seeing God as a fairy tale, see the Heavenly Father who truly knows you and desires a relationship with you. You don't have to be perfect to come to God; instead, you just have to come as you are with humility and repentance. Joe knows more than anyone. We all carry our baggage, but when we give our lives to God, we become a new creation in Him, and we are given a new heart for lov-ing God and loving others. He decided to name his new church *"Pursuing Freedom Non-Denominational Church"* because, as he discovered, only after giving one's life to Jesus can true freedom be found. He didn't want to get caught up with all the denomina-tion nonsense, and that is why he thought it was essential to have a non-denominational church.

Since Joe obtained his pastoral degree and opened the church, he felt blessed by the many people in the community who came to support the church and shared in his mission of spreading the love of God. Many of the kids he used to coach would come to his church with their families and commit their lives to Christ. Joe met this incredible young lady named Grace and her grandparents. Oh boy, did Grace have a story to tell. Grace lost her mother at childbirth, and her father left their family for the military, so she was raised by her grandparents. She had carried tremendous pain and guilt about the loss of her mother, and she faced abandonment issues about her father leaving her for the military. Grace knew that her parents believed in God, but she felt like all of God's grace had left the day she was born, and her mother died during her delivery. Grace always felt like she needed to make up for her mom's death, and if she were good enough, her father would come back to her. Still, after hearing the Gospel message in his church, she now has the love of her perfect and holy Heavenly Father and has received the ultimate love and the overflowing grace through Jesus Christ. One thing that blew Joe's mind was that when she joined the church's worship team, she insisted on bringing back an old hymn called "Amazing Grace." That hymn always brings tears to Joe's eyes because it was the one being sung that day he found God at church with Jimmy.

There was another lady that Joe met named Jannet, who was a single mother to a daughter named Lisa. She felt betrayed by her ex-husband, who left her and their daughter behind, choosing to take Lisa's twin brother with him as he pursued a career as an NBA coach. She then had to work her life away at Steele Manufacturing, feeling like she had to choose her job over being a mother to her own daughter, Lisa. Jannet fears that her daughter may have married the wrong person because she didn't have a good father figure in her life, and prays that her daughter can have a relationship with her Heavenly Father. She had asked Pastor Joe to meet with her daughter because Jannet really desires for Lisa to find the freedom that only comes from giving one's life to Jesus.

CHAPTER 11

The Night Before

J onathan had achieved success in so many areas of his life. As the CEO of his late father's company, Steele Manufacturing, he has made the business the most successful it has been since its inception. He was about to make a business deal that would double his profits, being the sole provider of military weapons in the entire state of Texas. Not only had he had success as CEO of Steele Manufacturing, but he had a wife who was his high school sweetheart, and they had three incredible children. Jonathan was more than capable of providing a comfortable life for his family. The only thing is, no matter how successful he had become, his marriage felt more strained than ever. His wife, Lisa, had been on a God-kick that she wouldn't let go of. He knew that was because of her mother, who had been nagging her to go to church. They used to have fun together, but now anything he does seems to irritate her.

On top of that, every day that he walks into work, he passes by a blind homeless man who always smiles at him and holds a sign that reads *"I once was blind but now I see. Would you please help me?"* That sign always irritated Jonathan. First of all, how stupid that the sign says that he now sees when he was a blind homeless man. He is as blind as a person could be.

On top of that, he always has a big smile on his face and says to him, *"God bless you!"* Jonathan thought to himself, *"If God is going to bless me the way He blessed you, I'd rather He not bless me; I'll bless myself with hard work."* He had a tough time believing that there is such a thing as a "good God." Not since he lost two friends and both his parents all in one year. There's no way a "good God" would allow that. But then there's a part of him that remembers Scrawny J and that miraculous touchdown he scored in that championship game. There was something profound about that game, and everyone knew it. But why in the hell would a "good God" allow Tommy Johnson and Jeffrey Thomson, two of the four members of the Quadruple Threat, who were young men in their prime, to die in a car accident while his friend Bobby Holt and he were able to survive?

On top of that, he had also lost his father and his mother about a week apart from each other. It still haunts him to this day that he never made his father proud. Jonathan loved his family and his children, but deep inside, he never allowed himself to get close to anyone, even his wife and children, because, honestly, he never felt like he deserved any of it. With his daughter's birthday coming up tomorrow, it's not like he doesn't want to give her a good birthday. He also doesn't love that he isn't close to his children. However, he was first going to have to celebrate the business deal after the big meeting to finalize the agreement, which would make Steele Manufacturing the sole provider of weapons in the Texas military. The deal was nearly finalized, but they just have to dot the i's and cross the t's in this business meeting tomorrow. Of course, he will have to deal with his wife, Lisa, tonight. She's gonna hound him on making it to their daughter, Jessica-Ann's, birthday party tomorrow night. Of course, he wants to be there and spend time with Jessica-Ann and their sons, Tommy and Jeffrey, but he hates the constant nagging from his wife. She was always complaining about how he had not been home to be the father and husband that they deserved. It's not like he's running a multimillion-dollar company and hasn't provided for his family or anything. But before he was going to deal with all that drama at home, he was going to have a few drinks at the local bar. He missed the days when he and his wife, Lisa, would have drinks and cigarettes together at the campfire, but those days felt like a lifetime ago, so instead, he was going to do that with the boys at the bar.

Most days, Lisa just felt like giving up, crying herself to sleep. She missed who her husband used to be. She missed feeling loved and being seen. Nowadays, they may share a bed at night, but more often than not, he passes out on the living room couch, and she has to clean up after him and explain to their kids that he's just tired from work. She loves their kids, and she still loves and cares for Jonathan, her husband, but he is no longer the person he used to be. It's like he gave up on trying to be real to himself and gave himself to his work and to the bottle. Not to say that she never wanted a drink herself. She often reminisces about the campfires, the cigarettes, and the conversations they used to have. Still, now it's as if he has given up on the marriage and thinks that providing financially is what a husband and father should do, nothing more, nothing less. She is grateful for the home they have, for their beautiful children, and for the home that Jonathan provided for her mother, but she can't raise this family on her own. Their kids need their father present, and she needs her husband.

The only thing that has kept her sane is her conversations with her mother, who encouraged her and gave her messages from the Bible. Recently, Lisa has started attending a new church with the kids, called "Pursuing Freedom Non-Denominational Church." She has also been meeting with Pastor Joe. Little does her husband know, but Pastor Joe was Jonathan's high school football coach, and she didn't want to use that information to manipulate him into going to church. Still, she gained a deeper understanding of Jonathan from Pastor Joe, and she has been gaining a greater insight into God and faith. She has not been able to bring herself to come to faith because of the heartache that her marriage has given her. She often told her mom and Pastor Joe that it would take a miracle to bring her husband back, and she believes that is the miracle it would take to get her to come to faith.

However, hearing the Gospel, attending church, and talking with her mom and Pastor Joe have really been the saving grace in helping her navigate life. To her surprise, her kids also enjoy church. This church is unlike any church experience she has ever had. It didn't feel judgmental or cliquey, but it is loving, supportive, and genuinely cares for the people in the congregation. There was something beautiful about this church. The messages always express that you don't need to be good enough for God, that God loves you as you are, and He wants a genuine relationship with you. That is a God that she could see herself believing in. She has always been about inclusion and an advocate for the marginalized, and that seems to be the message that was shared in the life of Jesus. Lisa is desperate for that kind of relationship with God, but she can't bring herself to believe it while Jonathan is deeply hurting and deeply hurting the family. She knows that hurt people hurt people, and that is what her husband is doing. Tomorrow is their daughter, Jessica-Ann's, birthday celebration at the local pizza buffet restaurant in town, and all she wants Jonathan to do is bring her birthday present to the party and be on time. However, she fears that this is too much to ask and that she will be let down once again. Lisa knew that tomorrow was also the day of the big business deal for Steele Manufacturing, and that business had become his life. She feared he would prioritize his business over his family, as he had done for years.

That evening, the evening before the big day of the birthday party for Jessica-Ann and the big business deal for Steele Manufacturing, Jonathan came home, stumbling drunk from a night out with the boys at the bar. Lisa just broke down in anger and started yelling at Jonathan. She yelled at him, saying, "You know that tomorrow is your daughter's birthday, and you just do whatever you want. You are never here for your family. You are always drinking with the boys. What about being a husband and father to your family?! You are just being like the asshole father and husband that your father was!" That line cut Jonathan deeply. It really exposed the deep cut in his heart. Jonathan never let go of the hurt his father had caused him. In hurt and anger, Jonathan yelled back and said, "You know better than to utter one single bad word against my father, you bitch!" After he said that, he slapped her across the face. He had never hit Lisa before. He looked at his hand and couldn't believe he just did that.

Lisa was in shock. He had never hit her; this was not the kind of person Jonathan was. She yelled at him, as she shoved the present into Jonathan's chest, saying, "Bring this present to the restaurant at 7 p.m. for your daughter. If you are not there at 7 with that present, I AM DONE!" She then went to their bedroom and started sobbing in bed. She didn't know what to do, but she called Pastor Joe. She was deeply shocked and deeply hurt.

Jonathan couldn't believe what he had just done. He left the house and went to his car and cried out to his dad, saying, *"Why did you do this to me? Why did you not love me? Why am I never enough?"*

CHAPTER 12

The Big Incident

Pastor Joe, Jimmy Jones, and Grace

Friday morning, Grace was really excited to connect her newly found father with her pastor. Little did she know that Pastor Joe and her father had a more complicated history than she ever realized. Pastor Joe always preached about not needing to be good enough for God, but to come to Him as you are in faith. God loves each and every one of us unconditionally and desires a relationship with all of us; we simply need to recognize that we are lost and in need of a Savior. God loved us so much that He gave His one and only Son to die for us for our sins. She recently found her father in his lowest state, being blind and attempting suicide by jumping off a bridge. It could be nothing else but God's hand in this situation when she found him at that exact moment. Afterward, they would go for lunch and coffee once a week at the coffee shop where they had met the night before. This morning, her father was willing to meet with her and her pastor at the same coffee shop. She was beyond excited. She always thought it was weird that he never offered to bring her to his place, and he always seemed unkempt, but she couldn't judge him. She had to deal with a lot of trauma and a lot of healing throughout her life because she believed that her father never wanted her. At times, her emotions, if left unchecked, could still bring up bitterness, but from what she has seen, he has been just as broken, if not more so, than she, and it was a blessing that God brought them together.

At 10:00 a.m., Grace arrived at the coffee shop, and Pastor Joe was waiting at a table. She came up to him and hugged him. She thanked him for being willing to meet with her and her father today. About a minute later, her father walked in. To her surprise, Pastor Joe was completely shocked. He asked Grace if this was her father, and she nodded her head yes. She went up to her dad and hugged him. Pastor Joe took a minute before he could do anything. Finally, he came up and said to her father, "Jimmy Jones?! There's no way! It's been years! How are you, brother?" Her father responded, "Coach Joe?" His eyes started to tear up, "Is it really you?" They hugged each other, and her pastor responded to her dad, saying in a voice filled with crying laughter, "People call me Pastor Joe now!" They laughed despite having teary eyes. Grace asked them, "Do you guys know each other?"

Pastor Joe responded, "Your dad was a part of the high school football team that I coached, and he is really the reason that I found my faith." Grace was in complete awe. She could not help but realize that God was at the center of everything. She started getting happy tears and gave both her father and Pastor Joe a big group hug. After they each had their dose of sappiness, they ordered their coffee and breakfast and sat at the table. Her father and Pastor Joe were explaining their past together, talking about the huge championship game, her dad's miraculous game-changing touchdown, and their experience of going to church together for the first time, where they both found God, and where her dad met her mother. Her father then explained to her and Pastor Joe what happened to his wife, Grace's mother, the pregnancy complications during childbirth, and how he decided to give their daughter a better life than he could provide, by giving their daughter to his wife's parents. He left to go overseas for the military, where he lost his vision after a bomb explosion. Jimmy did not want to tell his daughter or Joe that he was homeless, so he kept that quiet, but it felt good for him to get all the rest off his chest. He also explained how he lost faith after the horrors that he experienced in war, losing his wife and child, as well as his eyesight. He couldn't bring himself to believe in an all-loving and all-powerful God with what he had gone through. Jimmy explained how he fell deep into alcohol addiction, and the night that God sent his daughter to save him from his suicide attempt. It was in that moment that he felt God's presence again and was ready to surrender fully to God's plan. For all three of them, they could not believe how God had worked in their lives to bring about this full-circle moment. They all truly felt God's presence and God's love and grace in their lives. It was truly miraculous.

After they all went their separate ways from the coffee shop, Jimmy couldn't help but have the feeling that, after praying and thanking God for looking after him, his daughter, and Joe, there was a sense that God was going to do something life-changing today. After that beautiful experience, he couldn't help but say to God, "Here I am, Lord, my life is Yours, I fully trust in You." When he arrived at his usual street corner, he felt compelled to grab his sign, which read, *"I once was blind but now I see. Would you please help me?"* and pray for anyone he heard passing by while sitting on the street. With a grateful smile, Jimmy grabbed his sign and sat on the street corner, holding it in prayer and thanksgiving, smiling and waving to everyone who passed by.

Lisa Steele

The morning of Jessica-Ann's birthday party was off to a rough start. Lisa cried all night after the huge fight with her drunk husband. Jonathan had never hit her before. She couldn't help but visualize the darkness in his eyes when he slapped her across the face, calling her such a degrading name. This was not the man that she had married. He always had to deal with his internal trauma, but he knew that he could always confide in her. She was his safe space. But now she believes that to him, she just represents the family he never had, and it kills him inside. It's like he resents that he has a family that actually loves him because somewhere deep inside, he doesn't believe he deserves the life he has. She meant what she said that night; if Jonathan doesn't show up for their daughter's birthday party because he drank too much at their celebration party for the business deal, she will be done. As Pastor Joe said to her last night when she called in desperation, "You can't save anybody, only God can do that." That is the miracle she needs to see to believe. Jonathan's heart is so hardened from the trauma that he endured. She has constantly been reflecting on the quote, *"Hurt people hurt people."* That is 100 percent true. Sometimes the villain of the story doesn't want to be the villain, but the villain only knows how to live their life the way that they have been shown. Generational trauma can either destroy you or show you a better way, and unfortunately, her husband let the trauma destroy him. She has done everything she knew how to help him through his trauma and give him the love she has to offer, but you can't mend someone who doesn't want to be fixed. You can't love someone who believes they don't deserve to be loved. Jonathan has a wife and three children who love him to death and do everything they can to please him, but all their efforts are for naught because Jonathan would rather reside in the hell of his trauma than rise above with the life that is waiting for him with open arms. They say that hell is locked from within, and Jonathan is suffering within hell, tormented by his soul with no desire to unlock the gates of his own hell.

Jonathan Steele

The morning of his daughter's birthday and the biggest business deal of his life, Jonathan found himself waking up against his driver's side window with drool running down his face. He had the most significant headache from drinking the night before. His mind rushed with thoughts of how he hit his wife when he got home. How could he let himself get this low? He loved his family, he loved his wife, but something deep inside consistently brought him back to running drills all night long so that he could make his father proud. Everything he ever did was to make his father proud. No matter how hard he tried, he never heard those words from his dad: *"I'm proud of you, son."* He dreamed of those words every night, but every night his dreams turned to nightmares of his father kicking his ass and beating his mom after his dad had beaten him. Perhaps, if he had been enough for his old man, his old man would not have done those horrible things.

While he was in his thoughts, he heard his phone alarm sound off. Jonathan then had to get out of his car, go inside, and get ready for his day. As his old coach would say, it was time for him to shit, shave, and shower—the three S's. He then put on his best suit and grabbed his paperwork for the business meeting. Then, thinking of his nagging wife, remembered to grab Jessica-Ann's birthday present for the birthday party. He then headed back to his car, lit his lucky cigarette, and headed to work for the big payday he was about to receive.

On the way to his office, he saw the blind homeless man he had always seen. His sign really got under his skin today, for some reason, way more than usual. Sitting there with his sign and having the biggest smile on his face. *Who does this homeless man think he is?* Jonathan couldn't believe the audacity of the words of his sign, *"I once was blind but now I see. Would you please help me?"* The way his morning was going, he couldn't help but say this to the blind man in irritation, "No one is helping you, blind man." The blind man responded, "Maybe not, but God always does. God bless you, sir." Jonathan responded out of spite, "I promise you there is no God, definitely not a 'good' God." The blind man said, "I'm sorry you think that; I'll pray for you, good sir." Jonathan responded, "No thanks, I'm good. I'm gonna go make bank right now while you blindly beg for scraps." Jonathan then walked into the building to go to his meeting, while the blind man continued his huge, annoying smile.

Jonathan went into his office to prepare for the business meeting. If everything goes according to plan, Steele Manufacturing will be the sole provider of military weapons in all of Texas. This deal would double the company's production and profit. This would be the most significant increase in the company since his father's passing, and it would make Steele Manufacturing one of the top steel manufacturers in the United States. How could his dad not be proud of him for this? Before he went into the meeting, he poured a cup of coffee, and like he usually did, he mixed some whiskey into the coffee. Jonathan then went into the boardroom, where the meeting was being held, and excitedly shook the top Texas military general's hand, as well as everyone else in the room. Everyone held Jonathan up on a pedestal. He was 'THE' Jonathan Steele, the son of Frank Steele, the founder and original CEO of this fantastic organization. Once all of the greetings were made, everyone had a seat, and Jonathan stood at the head of the table. Jonathan gave his usual speech to the entire room. The head general addressed Jonathan with this: "Well, I for one love the steel that your old man produced, but how can we know that his son can repeatedly and efficiently create the same quality product at the best prices and with the quantity that this military needs?" With his confidence and arrogance, Jonathan responded while looking into the head general's eyes, "I promise you, even if there was a god, not even he could make steel as great as I can and as efficient as I have made this company." The general responded, "I have watched a lot of confident men in my day; never have I seen the amount of confidence you have in yourself and in your product that you have shown today. I'll be damned if I don't have respect for that kind of confidence. You, Mr. Jonathan Steele, you have yourself a deal." They shook hands, which signaled the finalization of the biggest deal that had ever been made in the history of Steele Manufacturing, and Jonathan had the biggest smile on his face. He finally felt like he accomplished something to be proud of, something his old man would be proud of.

After dotting the i's and crossing the t's on the paperwork for this business deal, Jonathan was ready to gather the boys to go to the bar and celebrate the historic agreement that had just been made. Everyone in the office was thrilled that the business deal had been finalized. Everyone was aware of the upcoming pay increases, and they were ready to celebrate. Right before they headed out to the local bar, Jonathan received a text from his wife saying, "Please don't forget your daughter's birthday party and her gift." Jonathan looked at the text and was annoyed. Of course, he won't forget; he didn't need a nagging text from his nagging wife. He was just going to have a few drinks and then head to the pizza restaurant.

When they arrived at the bar, Jonathan saw that his personal assistant had already ordered a line of shots for everyone. Jonathan hugged his assistant and said, "Hell yeah, let's party!" Then another coworker ordered a line, and then another, and then another. Everyone was having a ball! Then Jonathan had everyone compete in a beer-chugging contest, followed by another line of shots. Then another beer-chugging contest and another line of shots. Jonathan was no beginner at drinking, but within the first hour of being there, he was drinking at another level. He then stood up on the bar and gave a drunken toast to everyone at Steele Manufacturing, and everyone cheered his name! This was shaping up to be the wildest night of Jonathan's life.

A couple of hours later, amongst all the chaos, Jonathan received a text message from his wife, "Jonathan, it's 8 p.m. Your daughter's birthday party started an hour ago, and she is waiting for her dad and her birthday present." Dropping his beer glass, Jonathan woke up to the fact that he had gotten wasted drunk and was being a horrible father. All he could think to do was order water from the bartender and then get to that restaurant. But then he realized he had forgotten her birthday gift in his office. This is how he would make it up to her; he was going to get that present and be the knight in shining armor for his daughter. Jonathan Steele was now on a mission. He chugged that water down and got to his car.

When he sat down in his car, he realized how blurry his vision was from all those shots of whiskey. It took him three times to get his keys into the starter, and he realized that this was not going to be easy. In his drunkenness, Jonathan thought to himself, he's Jonathan Steele, the police got nothing on him. If anything, his taxes pay for the officer's yearly income. So, Jonathan decided to press on. As he attempted to drive, everything seemed to blur. He couldn't focus without his head hurting. He yelled at cars that honked at him, not knowing that he was swerving into the opposite lane. Finally, he was a block away from his office. He was going to quickly pull up, go in, grab the gift, and head to the restaurant.

Just as he was about to pull up to Steele Manufacturing, he noticed something, and then all of a sudden, there was a huge bump. There's no way that he could have run over something, is there? It was a significant enough bump that he got out of the car to see what had happened. In that moment, Jonathan realized he had made a huge mistake. A huge mistake. Underneath his car was the blind homeless man whom he always walked past, when heading into his office. Jonathan didn't know what to do but call his wife, "Lisa, I think I messed up really bad. I think I killed someone."

The cops were called. Jonathan was sitting on the street curb, consumed by guilt and stress. Flashbacks of the car accident that killed his friends in the Quadruple Threat, Tommy Johnson and Jeffrey Thomson, left him in horror. He also got flashbacks of finding out his father died and finding his mother dead.

When the cops arrived and put Jonathan in handcuffs, he realized that in his pursuit of being good enough, he had let everyone down. As he appeared to be successful, he had really become a failure. He failed his wife, his children, and his parents. He became the person that he had feared becoming.

Jonathan watched the police from the back of the cop car as they cleaned up the mess from the homeless man being hit by his own hands. Instead of bringing his daughter's birthday gift to her birthday party, he was arrested for killing a man in his drunken state. Words can't express the guilt that drowned his consciousness.

In his jail cell, Jonathan sat behind bars just like the emotional baggage that he had locked away since his parents passed. The guilt and the shame were drowning him, and instead of sharing his burdens with his wife, he buried his shame deeper and deeper, turning to substances instead of the people that he loved. Jonathan internally believed that he never deserved anything that he had ever received. He was able to marry his high school sweetheart, who truly loved him unconditionally. He acquired the position that his father held when he started Steele Manufacturing. Jonathan had so much, but the more he received, the more he resented himself. His whole life he had wanted to make his father proud, but no matter how much he accomplished, he would never hear the words from him that said, *"I'm proud of you, my son."* Those unspoken words haunted his soul forever.

The next morning, a police officer visited his cell and informed him that he had a visitor. Jonathan expected it to be his wife, Lisa. He figured she was coming to tell him that she wanted a divorce. He would not be able to blame her. He would attempt to beg for her back, but in his heart, he knew he didn't deserve her or his children. He failed them day after day, year after year. Yes, he was able to support them financially, but he was never a father to them, and he wasn't a husband to his wife. As far as he was concerned, he deserved to spend the rest of his life behind these bars. However, the cop told Jonathan that his visitor was the daughter of the victim that he killed. Her name was Grace, the daughter of Jimmy Jones. Jonathan thought to himself, *Jimmy Jones?* There is no way. Could the person that he killed really be Scrawny J from his high school football team? Could he really have killed the miracle player of the championship game? His heart just dropped. There is no way in hell that Scrawny J was the homeless man that he walked past every day going to work. The miracle maker who changed not only the championship game, but also his life. *How could Jimmy Jones go from being the star running back to a blind homeless man on the street?* He had so many questions. Could he really be Scrawny J from his high school football team? He could not live with himself for the way he treated that homeless man for years. If only he had known he was the miracle running back of the most important football game of his life.

The next thing Jonathan knew, a buzzer sounded, and in came the daughter of the man that he had just killed. The girl came in with tears running down her face. Through her tears, Jonathan saw Scrawny J in those eyes, and in that moment, he died inside. In that moment, he knew that he had killed the miracle running back of the championship game. The kid he had tormented throughout his school career was the same kid who showed up and won the most crucial game of the season. Jonathan Steele killed Scrawny J. Jimmy's daughter came in completely devastated. All she could do, all that she could handle, was go in, hand him a note, and run out. That thirty seconds of seeing Scrawny J's daughter come in, completely devastated from the loss of her father, hand her father's killer a note, and run out, will forever be ingrained in Jonathan's mind.

The effects of his horrible actions were shown to him in real time. Jonathan was shaking from the shame and guilt he had just felt. To be completely honest, he would rather die than exist in that moment ever again. He did not want to read what was inside that note. He couldn't imagine what could be in that note. More than likely, it shared how much of an evil person he was for taking away her father and the pain that she endured and would continue to endure, all because of him. He took the love of her father away from her. How could he bear to read the writing that was in this note? In utter anticipation, with all his strength and shaking hands, Jonathan opened the note that read, *"God still loves you, come back to Him."* He read that note and dropped it in complete and utter heartbreak. Tears started streaming down his face. In her pain, her devastation, she wanted to go to her father's killer and let him know that God loves him. There is no way in hell this is possible. There is no way in hell that a good God could love him with what he had done. There is no way . . . .

A few minutes later, which felt like an eternity in hell for Jonathan, the police officer returned and said, "You have another visitor." Jonathan, in the midst of personal hell and tears, insisted that he wasn't ready for another visitor. The police officer said, "You're gonna want to hear what this person has to say."

The next thing Jonathan saw was Coach Joe. He had to wipe his eyes to see if he was really seeing him. His hero, his coach. There is no way . . . In this moment. Coach Joe . . . .

CHAPTER 13

Jonathan Steele and Pastor Joe

Trying to wipe away the tears, Jonathan said to Coach Joe, "I don't know what to say, Coach. I messed up big time. I thought that I had it all. I had a career, I married my high school sweetheart, and I have three beautiful children, but I messed it all up. I always felt the need to be the best. I always needed to prove my worth, and now I feel worthless." Joe responded, "Now you feel worthless? I feel like that feeling isn't new, is it?" Jonathan answered, "I always wanted to make my old man proud. He was my idol, my superhero, my everything, and he never told me that he was proud of me. I guess I've always been chasing that, but it never happened."

Joe responded to Jonathan, "I always wanted to be in the NFL. It was my dream. Football was my life. Football was everything. Football became my god. But then, I had a career-ending injury, and football was no longer in the cards for me. I failed football. I failed my god. I'll be honest, there were times after that football injury that I wanted to end it all. My life, my worth, was tied to football, and when I no longer had it, I had nothing. I had no more dreams, no more goals, no more life in me. But then I had the opportunity to be a coach at your high school, so I swore to myself that I would be the best damn coach that a coach could ever be, and I planted my dream of the NFL into players that I really believed had a shot, and I pushed my dreams onto them. You were one of those players, Jonathan. I saw the way that your father treated you, and I saw you perform every action that you made as an attempt to be better than your old man, to prove him wrong. I don't think he ever was proud of you, because I believe he was never proud of himself. I don't think he had the capacity to offer his love to anyone because he never truly loved himself. I call that 'the family curse.' I believe you can never truly love your wife or children because you don't have love for yourself. You see, the Greatest Commandment tells us to love God with all that we are and love our neighbor as ourselves. Often, people will say, *'Love God and love people,'* but the problem with that is that *'Love God and love people'* is an incomplete quote. You can't love your neighbor if you don't love yourself. You can't pour into an empty cup from an empty cup. I don't want to get all religious on you, but because we are behind bars, maybe there's no better time. I have always been aware of God and the church, as I'm sure you have too. I mean, we are in a small Texas town in the Bible Belt. Every Sunday morning, hungover as someone can be, my parents made sure to get our butts to church. It was always preaching about the fires of hell and putting the fear of God in us. It was always intense, but that never got my old man to stop drinking or whipping us when we weren't good enough. Hell, oftentimes the pastor would be right alongside my old man at the bar on a Friday night after the high school football game. I also distinctly remember that in the living room of our house, there was an old picture of Jesus praying with an angelic halo around His head as He gazed towards the sky. That picture always creeped me out. I always believed that religion and God were a fairy tale that parents told their children to scare them into behaving. Kinda like the monster under your bed. But then a miracle happened. THE championship game. Your senior year's championship game. Many tragedies have befallen our town. Losing your old man and the loss of two members of our Quadruple Threat. Everything was stacked against us, and we were facing an impossible game in front of a community that desperately needed healing. This game was not just about us; it was for the healing of the entire community. Against all odds, in the midst of my giving up on our team, I sent in Scrawny J, and before every single person there, we witnessed a God-given miracle. Scrawny J ran past every single defender, scoring a 74-yard touchdown and eventually winning the championship game. In that moment, everything that I had ever believed came shattering down. God showed me in that moment that you don't need to be perfect to make a difference. You can be a scrawny kid, who seems like a nobody, and still win the championship game. Every single one of us treated that kid like dirt, and he was the sole reason we won that game. I believe that God has a sense of humor as He humbles us. The next Sunday, I went to church with Jimmy, and we both accepted Jesus into our hearts and into our lives. From that moment on, I knew I couldn't continue just teaching kids about football; I needed to share God's love and grace with everyone. I pursued a career as a pastor and started a church called "Pursuing Freedom Non-Denominational Church," where I had the opportunity to teach not perfection, but a call to God's love and truth in our lives. I want to share this Bible passage with you—Luke 15:4–7: "Which one of you, having a hundred sheep and losing one of them, does not leave the ninety-nine in the wilderness and go after the one that is lost until he finds it? When he has found it, he lays it on his shoulders and rejoices. And when he comes home, he calls together his friends and neighbors, saying to them, 'Rejoice with me, for I have found my sheep that was lost.' Just so, I tell you, there will be more joy in heaven over one sinner who repents than over ninety-nine righteous persons who need no repentance." Jesus loves each and every person enough that He, without question, will leave the ninety-nine to find and rescue you. We didn't deserve to be saved, but He came anyway. As it says in John 3:16: 'For God so loved the world that He gave His only Son, so that everyone who believes in Him may not perish but may have eternal life.' You see, Jonathan, we don't need to be perfect for God to love us; we just need to admit that we are lost and be willing to be rescued from our darkness. Ephesians 2:8–9 says, 'For by grace you have been saved through faith, and this is not your own doing; it is the gift of God—not the result of works, so that no one may boast.'" Joe then said, "You see, both of us have believed that we have to be perfect so that we can be loved and be seen, but God says that we don't need to be perfect, we just need to believe."

Trying to stop the tears, Jonathan replied, "I have never felt that kind of love. I don't even know what to say. I remember the feeling of the 74-yard touchdown from Scrawny J. There was something miraculous about that moment. I want that kind of love that you have, but I think I'm too far gone. I just killed the man that helped lead you to God, I killed the same Scrawny J that won that game for us. I killed the man that God used. I don't think that God will forgive me. I have been a horrible husband, a horrible father. I actually hit and swore at my wife. I have only cared for myself. I am a sinner deserving of hell. I deserve to rot in this prison cell."

Joe responded with, "Back in biblical times, there was this guy named Paul, who wrote a majority of the New Testament of the Bible. He is referred to as a 'saint' and a 'holy man.' But before he was a follower of Jesus Christ, he persecuted and killed Christians. He was actively trying to kill people who were serving Jesus. He said this in the book of 1 Timothy 1:12–17: 'I am grateful to Christ Jesus our Lord, who has strengthened me, because He judged me faithful and appointed me to His service, even though I was formerly a blasphemer, a persecutor, and a man of violence. But I received mercy because I had acted ignorantly in unbelief, and the grace of our Lord overflowed for me with the faith and love that are in Christ Jesus. The saying is sure and worthy of full acceptance, that Christ Jesus came into the world to save sinners—of whom I am the foremost. But for that very reason, I received mercy, so that in me, as the foremost, Jesus Christ might display the utmost patience, making me an example to those who would come to believe in Him for eternal life. To the King of the ages, immortal, invisible, the only God, be honor and glory forever and ever. Amen.'"

Not able to control his tears anymore, Jonathan responded, "I want that kind of love, Coach. What do I even do? What do I even say? I know I don't want to stay in this darkness anymore. I no longer want to prove my worth. It's killing me. Even worse than that, it's hurting the people that I love."

Joe responded, "If you want, I can lead you in a prayer. We can say these words, but none of this will mean anything if you don't believe these words in your heart. Are you ready to pray these words with belief?" Jonathan confirmed, "Yes, Coach, I'm ready."

Joe led Jonathan with this prayer, "God, I humbly come before You to say that I am sorry. I have tried to live this life in my own way, living for myself and for others. I have been broken and lost. I can't do this life anymore. I can't do this alone. Please forgive me. I believe that You are my Heavenly Father who sent Your Son to not only show me how to live, but died for me and defeated sin and death by His resurrection so that I may repent of my sinful ways and be born again in Him. I invite the Holy Spirit into my heart so that He can help guide me in the ways of Jesus and to live out the Greatest Commandment, loving God with all that I am and loving my neighbor as myself. I pray that I may begin my spiritual journey by walking in the ways of Jesus, letting go of my sins, and pursuing love and truth. I lay my life into Your hands, putting to death my sinful, selfish ways, and be born again through the Holy Spirit. In Jesus' name I pray, Amen."

After the prayer, Jonathan began to feel the Holy Spirit and experienced a profound sense of love that he had never imagined. All that he could do was physically fall to his knees and thank God. Jonathan had no idea where to even begin, but he knew that he wanted more. He wanted to do whatever he could to tell everyone what had happened to him at this moment. There was no greater feeling than the embrace of his Heavenly Father. He wanted validation from his broken and imperfect father, which he never received, but now he had gained unconditional love from the Creator of heaven and earth, the God who had created him. There were no words to describe this moment.

Once everything started to settle in, Pastor Joe shared this Bible verse with Jonathan—John 8:36: "So if the Son makes you free, you will be free indeed." After the Bible verse, Joe said this to Jonathan, "Jonathan. I want to be very clear. What you did was horrible. Every sin was a hammer-hit that nailed Jesus to that cross. There are consequences to our mistakes. Your family has suffered without having a man of God, a loving husband, and a present father. There is now a daughter without her earthly father because of the choices that you have made. As it says in the first part of Romans 6:23: 'For the wages of sin is death,' but the good news of the Gospel is said in the second part of that verse, 'but the free gift of God is eternal life in Christ Jesus our Lord.' I know that you have felt the weight of your sin, and now I want to offer you the grace that only comes from our Heavenly Father. I don't want your family to suffer any more than they already have. Lisa deserves the love of her husband, and your children deserve the presence of their loving father. I pray that you will cherish this moment so that you can live the rest of your life loving God and loving people. I have paid your bail so that you can come home to your family and be the man of God that He created you to be."

Jonathan, drowning in tears, muttered these words, "I don't deserve this, I don't deserve any of this. What can I say? What can I do to even begin to thank you?" Pastor Joe responded, "Just spread the Good News, my brother, and maybe attend my church, haha." He joked while giving Jonathan a friendly nudge on the shoulder.

The officer then came in and brought out Jonathan to be released. The first person Jonathan saw was the only other surviving member of the Quadruple Threat, Bobby Holt. Bobby had achieved the position of Chief of Police in their town and permitted the bail that Joe had submitted on Jonathan's behalf. Bobby had reconnected with Coach Joe as he started attending Pursuing Freedom Non-Denominational Church and gave his life to Christ. Jonathan was in complete shock until he saw his family, his loving wife Lisa, and their three children, Tommy, Jeffrey, and Jessica-Ann. Through the tears, Jonathan kneeled before his wife and said, "I don't even know where to begin. I have truly been a failure as a husband, as a father, and as a human being. I don't have the words to express how sorry I am. All I know is that I love you, and I will live every day for the rest of my life attempting to make it up to you." Lisa, through her tears, responded, "You don't know how tempted I have been to give up on you, and then this. I have been praying to God that if He is real, I will believe when I see your hard heart soften. You don't know this, but all of us out here were able to hear every word in that cell, and God showed me a truly repentant heart, and I now believe. If God can heal you, He can heal anybody. I have missed you, the real you, for years. You have pursued your business, your dead father's acceptance, for so many years, while you overlooked your true family. I want the real you. The you that I spent prom night with. The you at the campfires. The you that loved me. I want the man who wants to be the father who loves his children and is proud of them. I want you, you big idiot. I love you, Jonathan, and I am ready to walk hand in hand on our spiritual journey, walking in the footsteps of our Savior Jesus Christ. I am ready to give Jesus my life and give you my heart all over again." Through the tears, Jonathan and Lisa shared the most heartbreakingly beautiful kiss that anyone could ever see. He then turned to his children, saying, "Tommy and Jeffrey, I am sorry that I only cared about football in your lives. I don't even know if you guys even like football. I apologize for pushing my agenda onto you. Can you forgive me, my little buddies?"

Tommy and Jeffrey replied, "We love football, Dad, we would just love it more with you in it with us. You'll always be our number one, Dad." In full smiles, Jonathan hugged Tommy and Jeffrey. He then turned to his daughter, Jessica-Ann. He looked into her eyes that were obviously hurt and said to her, "Jessica-Ann, my little princess. I am so, so sorry that I missed your birthday. I am so, so sorry that I haven't treated you like the beautiful princess that you are. I really, really want to make it up to you. Will you please forgive Daddy?" Jessica-Ann's frown turned into the happiest smile a little girl could have, and she said, "Yes, Daddy, I love you." And he embraced her with the biggest hug, telling her, "I love you, my beautiful princess."

After all the heartwarming conversations and loving embraces, Jonathan walked hand in hand with his loving wife and beautiful children, as they headed to their car, thanking God and ready to embark on a new adventure of loving God and loving each other. There was something brighter about that sunny day. Pastor Joe stood with Bobby Holt and watched the brand-new joy and love of this beautiful family. As they were witnessing this special moment, Bobby asked Pastor Joe, "There is something truly special about the power of redemption by the grace of God, isn't there?"

Paster Joe replied, "Something truly special indeed. What the adversary intends for harm, the Heavenly Father will use for good. As the beautiful hymn goes, *'I once was lost, but now I'm found; was blind, but now I see.'* We all have been lost, but when we find Jesus, we are truly found."

Conclusion

Once, in a small town rich in history, there was an old, simple married couple. They didn't have a lot, but they had each other and they had their God.

In a world full of so much hate and division, in a world that is so busy and lacking human connection, I couldn't help but wonder how this couple could be so full of love, compassion, grace, and peace. How could they have so much joy and laughter while just sitting on their porch day after day? There was something mysterious and different about this couple. Some kind of eternal light that shines through the darkness. They were obviously not perfect, but their presence overflowed with joy, love, and peace. They didn't concern themselves with the divisiveness of politics or the economy. They didn't see anyone based on their appearance or beliefs. They welcomed everyone with open arms and compassionate conversations. They had no concern about differences; they treated everyone as children of God. No matter who you were or how many people were there, they always made sure to welcome each and every person, welcoming them to the table with a hot, juicy burger and a cold beverage. They cared about each and every conversation. I can't help but think the world would be a much better place if everyone were like this older couple. Not concerned with social media. Not concerned about their wealth or status. Not concerned about your appearance or beliefs. There was always a seat at their table. There was something so special and inspiring about being at this old couple's house—Mr. and Mrs. Steele.

As a visitor at their table, I couldn't help but ask about their secret to a successful marriage and their sense of overwhelming peace. Mrs. Steele replied, "Every day we choose to live a life of compassion, grace, love, and peace because we know the price of living a life full of selfishness, pride, division, and sin. It's not always easy, but we know it's the only life worth living." In agreement, Mr. Steele also responded, "I tried living a life full of ego and pride and almost lost everything. Only after letting go can you receive the blessings that fulfill. There's an old hymn that says, *'I once was lost, but now I'm found; was blind, but now I see.'* I believe there's nothing truer than that. An old friend taught me that."

After hearing their responses, they offered me a large, juicy, delicious burger, along with an ice-cold beverage. I then asked, "Before we drink and indulge in this delicious meal, can the man of the house offer a meaningful toast?" Mr. Jonathan Steele laughed and said, "You betcha, my brother. Here's to a life full of grace, love, and some football!"

The End.